READING INTO CHINA

漫读中华

历史故事

HISTORICAL STORIES

总主编◎刘　军

主　编◎王　斌　姚鹏飞

编　者◎耿小敏　蒋婷婷　包路加

外语教学与研究出版社
FOREIGN LANGUAGE TEACHING AND RESEARCH PRESS
北京 BEIJING

图书在版编目（CIP）数据

历史故事 ：英、汉 / 王斌，姚鹏飞主编 ；耿小敏等编．-- 北京 ：外语教学与研究出版社，2018.7（2023.7 重印）
（漫读中华 / 刘军总主编）
ISBN 978-7-5213-0289-9

Ⅰ．①历… Ⅱ．①王… ②姚… ③耿… Ⅲ．①汉语－对外汉语教学－语言读物 Ⅳ．①H195.5

中国版本图书馆 CIP 数据核字（2018）第 175695 号

出 版 人　王　芳
项目策划　黄　骥
责任编辑　张荣婕
责任校对　黄　骥
装帧设计　黄　浩
出版发行　外语教学与研究出版社
社　　址　北京市西三环北路 19 号（100089）
网　　址　https://www.fltrp.com
印　　刷　天津市光明印务有限公司
开　　本　787×1092　1/16
印　　张　10.5
版　　次　2018 年 8 月第 1 版　2023 年 7 月第 7 次印刷
书　　号　ISBN 978-7-5213-0289-9
定　　价　49.90 元

如有图书采购需求，图书内容或印刷装订等问题，侵权、盗版书籍等线索，请拨打以下电话或关注官方服务号：
客服电话：400 898 7008
官方服务号：微信搜索并关注公众号“外研社官方服务号”
外研社购书网址：https://fltrp.tmall.com

物料号：302890001

记载人类文明
沟通世界文化
www.fltrp.com

序

束定芳教授

中华优秀传统文化是中华民族代代相传的丰富遗产，是中华民族对人类文明的伟大贡献。随着国际文化交流的不断深入，逐渐加强中华优秀传统文化在语言教学中的融入，对促进跨文化交际具有重要的意义。在此背景下，“漫读中华”（*Reading into China*）系列丛书的推出应该是传承中华优秀传统文化、推进其国际传播的一次有益尝试。

Reading into China，可以理解为以阅读的方式走进中华民族文化；其中的*into*是一个动态介词，意在帮助读者全面地、深入探究式地、由古及今地认识和了解中华文化。丛书的中文名是“漫读中华”，以“漫”的方式阅读中华文明，品味中华文化的博大精深。

“漫读中华”系列丛书在内容上，从物态文化、制度文化、行为文化和心态文化等角度取材，体现了广义文化的内涵和外延。丛书在文本架构上以“中国故事”为着眼点，用文化链接的方式介绍了相关的中华优秀传统文化亮点，并与外国文化进行对比阅读，以此促进双向跨文化交际，帮助读者认识和了解中华民族文化，领悟中华文化和世界文化在形成和发展过程中的相互作用和各自特点，增强文化认同。

很多中华文化的表现形式是非文本的。“漫读中华”系列丛书在形式编排上注重图文并茂，使阅读内容更为直观和形象。所选图片包括典籍、画作、碑文等文化遗物，多选自于博物馆展品或藏品，通过图释及相关阅读内容赋予这些陈列品鲜活的生命力，展现文物背后的文化内涵；也包括故居、古城、宫殿等文化遗迹，通过对相关故事或文化现象的阐述，增强读者对文化名胜的认知，让读者有身临其境的文化体验；还包括民俗、民间艺术、传统仪式等文化行为的图片，体现民族和区域特色的行为模式。

总之，“漫读中华”系列丛书有介绍、有对比，有梳理、有分析，有传承、有创新，是一套颇具特色的教材，也是一套深入浅出的文化普及读本。丛书的编写团队是一支勤勉钻研、善于思考，并对文化、语言和教学研究满含热情的中青年学者队伍。中华优秀传统文化的继承和传播需要这种钻研、思考和热情。

2018年8月3日
于上海

束定芳，上海外国语大学教授，博士生导师，上海外国语大学附属中学现任校长；外语类核心刊物《外国语》主编，海外语言学核心期刊*Journal of Pragmatics*等刊物编委；同时担任中国认知语言学研究会会长，全国高校外语学刊研究会秘书长。

前言

中华优秀传统文化是中华民族集体智慧的结晶，是人类文明的源头之一。讲好中国故事是新时代中国特色社会主义的命题和使命。“漫读中华”系列丛书以“源于中国，属于世界，基于历史，引领未来”为指导思想，使学习者在阅读故事的过程中理解中华优秀传统文化的内涵和表现形式，为用英语讲述中国故事、在国际交往中传承并弘扬中华优秀传统文化奠定基础。本系列丛书适合国内中、高级英语语言和文化学习者使用，亦适合对中国文化感兴趣的外国学习者使用；可用于课堂教学及学生课外自主学习。

本系列丛书包含历史故事、古代神话、民间传说和文学经典四个分册。丛书内容具有以下特点。

1. 选材广泛。丛书选材涵盖从远古到近代的哲学、科学、文学、医学、艺术等主题，选用能够展示中华民族智慧、勇敢、谦逊、礼让、大义等中华优秀传统文化的故事。

2. 结构合理。每个分册包含二十个单元。每个单元包括引言、故事、文化链接、讨论四个部分。故事内容短小精悍，采用图文结合的编写形式，符合现代阅读习惯。

3. 双语编写。采用英文和中文双语编写，方便课堂教学、自主学习和拓展阅读等。

4. 视角新颖。每个单元都编写了数条文化链接，通过扩充与故事相关的中华传统文化知识以及对比中外文化等内容，以点带面，提高学习者关于中华文化主题的语言应用能力和跨文化交际能力。

5. 思辨培养。每个单元均设计了思辨讨论，帮助学习者深入理解和分析中华优秀传统文化的内涵和特点，领悟中华文化在世界文化的形成和发展过程中发挥的重要作用。思辨讨论题亦可以作为演讲、辩论和写作等学习任务的主题。

“漫”本义指水向四面八方流淌，本丛书所有作者希望以中国故事为源头，链接中华文化，连贯中西文化本源，并希冀中华优秀传统文化在国际上的传播蓬勃发展，无远弗届。

Contents
目录

I 壹 Yu the Great Controlling the Waters 001

大禹巧治黄河水 005

II 贰 Never Feeling Embarrassed to Ask a Lesser Person 009

不耻下问 013

III 叁 Legendary Physician Bian Que 017

神医扁鹊 021

IV 肆 Mao Sui Recommending Himself 025

毛遂自荐 029

V 伍 Xiang Yu Cutting off All His Means of Retreat 033

项羽破釜沉舟 037

VI 陆 Cai Lun Inventing Paper 041

蔡伦造纸 045

VII 柒 Kong Rong Yielding Bigger Pears 049

孔融让梨 053

VIII 捌 Three Visits to the Thatched Cottage 057

三顾茅庐 060

IX 玖 Wang Xizhi Being Fond of Geese 063

王羲之爱鹅 068

X 拾 Xie Daoyun Comparing Snowflakes to Willow Catkins 073
谢道韫咏絮 077

XI 拾壹 Zu Chongzhi and *Pi* 081
祖冲之与圆周率 085

XII 拾贰 Dance of Rainbow Skirt and Feathered Gown 089
霓裳羽衣舞 093

XIII 拾叁 Lu Yu Distinguishing Water 097
陆羽辨水 101

XIV 拾肆 Sima Guang Breaking the Vat 105
司马光砸缸 109

XV 拾伍 Su Shi Taking the Imperial Examination 113
苏轼科考 117

XVI 拾陆 Temujin's Horse-Racing Strategy 121
铁木真赛马 125

XVII 拾柒 Marco Polo Traveling to China 129
马可波罗在中国 133

XVIII 拾捌 Zheng He to the Western Ocean 137
郑和下西洋 141

XIX 拾玖 The Story of *Kangxi Dictionary* 145
《康熙字典》的故事 149

XX 廿 Destruction of Opium at Humen 153
虎门销烟 157

I YU THE GREAT CONTROLLING THE WATERS

Introduction

Yu the Great (around 2200 BC–2101 BC) is said to establish the Xia Dynasty, traditionally considered the first dynasty of China.

According to Sima Qian's famous *Records of the Grand Historian*, Yu was Gun's son; Gun was the son of Emperor Zhuanxu; Zhuanxu's father, Changyi, was the son of the Yellow Emperor. The Yellow Emperor was called one of the ancestors of Chinese civilization.

⊙ The stone carved with a pattern of an agricultural tool *leicha* used in Yu's controlling the waters, found at Mount Juci in Yuzhou in Henan Province

⊙ The image of Yu grasping a *leicha* to control the waters in a copy of a stone rubbing, found at Wu's Clan Temple in Jiaxiang in Shandong Province

Story Time

More than four thousand years ago, the Chinese heartland frequently suffered from floods. Yu's father, Gun, was assigned with designing a system to control the waters. He spent more than nine years building a series of dikes and dams along the riverbanks, but all of them were ineffective. Yu then had orders to continue his father's work.

Yu started with making a careful study of the river systems and attempted to find out why his father's great efforts had failed.

One day, he found a stream running through the high mountains which looked like the natural barriers to the waters. "How could the stream keep flowing freely through such barriers?" Yu was lost in thought. Gazing at the flowing water and the gaps between mountains, he had an idea. Instead of directly damming the rivers' flow, he created a system of irrigation canals which led floodwater into fields. At the same time, he made great efforts to remove mud and stones from the riverbeds.

Yu's efforts were successful, which also allowed ancient Chinese culture to flourish along the Yellow River, the Wei River, and other waterways of the Chinese heartland. The project made Yu well known throughout China's history and become one of the few Chinese rulers named with the title "Great."

⊙ Yu's Gateway in Shaanxi Province, named for Yu's leading the workers to open up this channel which blocked water from flowing

Cultural Links

The origin of *Huaxia*

Huaxia refers to the Chinese nation. The characters of "Hua" and "Xia" were a pair of synonyms in ancient China.

According to historical texts, the Xia as a tribe was said to develop around the time of Emperor Zhuanxu. As Yu controlled the flood successfully, he took over the throne from Shun and established the Xia Dynasty (2070 BC–1600 BC). It started a period of family or clan control, spanning four thousand years or so.

Records of the Grand Historian

Records of the Grand Historian is a historical work finished by Sima Qian in the Han Dynasty. The work covers the history of a 3,000-year period from the age of the legendary Yellow Emperor to the reign of Emperor Wu of Han.

In the West, historical works were used to treat history as a continuous or sweeping narrative. *Records of the Grand Historian* set a new model of breaking it up into the overlapping units dealing with famous figures and significant events.

The Nine Provinces

Yu's experience in controlling the waters is said to have made him know very well about all regions of what was then Han Chinese territory. According to the "Yu Gong Treatise" in the *Book of Documents*, Yu divided the Chinese "world" into nine provinces. The term has now come to be one of the symbolic names for China.

The flood narrative in the *Epic of Gilgamesh*

The flood narrative may provide some insight into the formation and development of different cultures. In the *Epic of Gilgamesh*, which is regarded as the earliest surviving great work of literature, Tablet XI contains a flood story.

It tells that the gods decided to send a great flood. However, a god wanted to save Utnapishtim and instructed him to build a giant ship. With his great effort, the ship was completed. On this ship, Utnapishtim and his entire family, together with his craftsmen and all the animals of the field, survived the waters.

◎ Tablet XI of the *Epic of Gilgamesh*, held by the British Museum in London, the United Kingdom

Discussion

1. Why do you think Yu could control the waters successfully?
2. Do you know any other flood narratives? Try to tell what you know.

壹　大禹巧治黄河水

引

据说大禹（公元前 2200 年—公元前 2101 年）建立了中国第一个朝代——夏朝。

根据司马迁的《史记》所著：禹之父曰鲧，鲧之父曰帝颛顼，颛顼之父曰昌意，昌意之父曰黄帝。黄帝被称为“中华文明始祖之一”。

⊙ 大禹治水农具“耒锸”的石刻图样
发现于河南禹州具茨山

⊙ 大禹手持“耒锸”治水的石拓画
发现于山东嘉祥武氏祠

故事

在4000多年前，中华的中原地带常有水患，禹的父亲鲧奉命治水。鲧用了九年多时间在大河两岸筑起许多堤坝，但都没有达到很好的治水效果。之后，由其子禹继承治水大任。

禹首先对河水体系作了一番严密的考察，寻求自己父亲竭尽全力但还是以失败告终的问题所在。

一天，他在崇山峻岭中发现一条溪水奔流不息，这些山脉犹如阻止水流的天然屏障。"为何在这样的屏障之间，水流还能自由流动不停息？"禹陷入了沉思。凝视着水流和山间的那些山口，他想到了一个办法。一改直接"堵"住河水的方法，他设计了用于灌溉的沟渠体系，可以将洪水引入田地，同时又能将河床中的淤泥和石头沉淀掉。

禹治水成功了，也使得古代中华文化在黄河、渭河和中原地带的其他流域繁荣起来。治水使禹在中国历史上相当知名，并使禹成为被尊称为"大"的少有的几位统治者之一。

◎ 陕西 “禹门口”
因大禹带领众人在此凿开堵住水流的山口而得名

文化链接

“华夏”的起源

“华夏”现被用来指代中国。“华”和“夏”在古代中国被用作一组同义词。

据史书所述，夏作为部族约在颛顼做首领时期发展起来。由于禹治水成功，他继位于舜，当了部落首领并建立了夏朝（公元前2070年—公元前1600年），开启了大约四千年的家族世袭制。

《史记》

《史记》是由汉朝司马迁完成的历史巨著，记载了从传说中黄帝时代开始至汉武帝时代的三千年历史。

西方撰写历史作品常运用连贯的通史叙述方式，而《史记》按著名人物和重要事件分类，将历史分解成相互交叠的片段，建立了一种新体裁。

九州

据说大禹治水的经历使他对之后的汉族疆域所有地区都非常了解。据《尚书·禹贡》记载，大禹将“天下”分为九州。“九州”现已成为象征中国的代称之一。

《吉尔伽美什史诗》中的洪水故事

通过洪水故事，我们可以深入了解不同文化的形成和发展。《吉尔伽美什史诗》被认为是现存最古老的文学巨著，其中的第11块泥板讲述了一则洪水故事。

诸神决定降临一场大洪水，而一位主神想要救乌塔那匹兹姆，于是就教他建造一艘大船。经过不懈努力，终于造船成功。乌塔那匹兹姆和他所有的家人、工匠们以及所有田地里的动物，乘坐这艘船在洪水中存活了下来。

◎《吉尔伽美什史诗》的第11块泥板
英国伦敦大英博物馆展品

讨论

1. 你认为禹为什么能成功治理水患?
2. 你还知道其他的洪水故事吗？请试着讲一下。

II NEVER FEELING EMBARRASSED TO ASK A LESSER PERSON

Introduction

Confucius (551 BC–479 BC) was a Chinese philosopher, educator and statesman of the Spring and Autumn Period in China's history. The philosophy of Confucius, also known as Confucianism, emphasizes humaneness, righteousness, propriety, moral wisdom and faithfulness.

Throughout the history, Confucius is widely considered one of the most important individuals who affect people's behavior. His philosophy has a profound influence on the people in East Asia and other parts of the world.

⊙ The picture of Confucius in the *Traces of Sage*, painted by Qiu Ying of the Ming Dynasty

◉ The largest Confucian Temple in China, located in Qufu in Shandong Province

Story Time

In spite of being considered one of the most knowledgeable people during the Spring and Autumn Period, Confucius was humble with an inquiring mind.

One day, Confucius paid a visit to the Imperial Ancestral Temple of the Lu State to commemorate the late kings. Surprisingly, he asked about almost every detail of the ceremony. Some people laughed at him and said, "Who says the sage knows everything? He even knows nothing about a memorial ceremony."

"The reason why I know more is that I would ask questions about whatever I don't completely understand," answered Confucius.

A few days later, Confucius and his students arrived in the Wei State, where Kong Yu, an official of that state, was given the title of *Wen* after his death and therefore referred to an honorific title as *Kong Wenzi*.

Zi Gong, a student of Confucius, did not think Kong Yu deserved that title. He asked, "Although Kong Yu was competent, there were more capable officials in the Wei State. Moreover, he made many mistakes when alive. Why could he have such an honorific title after his death?"

"Because he was bright and loved learning, never feeling embarrassed to ask a lesser person," said Confucius.

Cultural Links

Zi and the *Hundred Schools of Thoughts*

In ancient China, *Zi* was an honorific title used after the surname, referring to the philosophers with moral integrity, profound knowledge or high social status. It means "master" as in Kongzi and Laozi.

The Spring and Autumn Period (770 BC–476 BC), when Confucius and Laozi lived, began a golden age of Chinese philosophy. The *Hundred Schools of Thoughts* is a name given to philosophers and schools that flourished in this age before the Qin Dynasty. The phenomenon has been called the *Contention of a Hundred Schools of Thoughts*. Among them, the most influential schools of thoughts included Confucianism, Legalism, Daoism, Mohism, School of Yin-yang and etc.

Analects

The *Analects* is a documented collection of sayings from Confucius and some of his contemporaries, which is believed to have been compiled by the followers of Confucius. Over the past two thousand years, the *Analects*, where Confucianism is faithfully represented, has been one of the most influential books around the world.

◎ *Analects*, held by the Sungkyunkwan University Museum in Seoul, South Korea

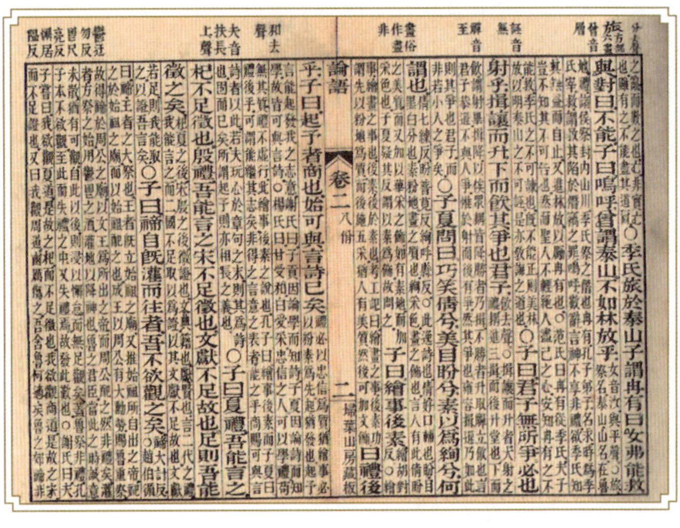

◎ A page from the *Analects*

◉ The sculptures of Confucius (left of center), Moses (center) and Solon (right of center), forming the central group over the eastern entrance of the Supreme Court Building in the United States

Confucius' sculpture in the Building of the Supreme Court of the United States

Over the eastern entrance of the Supreme Court Building in the United States, the sculpture of Confucius, together with that of Moses, who introduced Ten Commandments, and that of Solon, the Greek lawgiver, can be seen as a group in the center. The designer would like to express the idea that American legal system was derived from former civilizations. Confucius, Moses and Solon are chosen to represent three eastern civilizations which have had a great impact on the development of American law.

Discussion

1. How did Confucius become more knowledgeable, according to the story?
2. If there is something you do not understand, will you feel embarrassed to ask anyone else, including a lesser person? State your reasons.

贰　不耻下问

引

孔子（公元前551年—公元前479年）是中国春秋时期思想家、教育家和政治家，其思想又称“儒家思想”，倡导仁、义、礼、智、信。

孔子是一位受普遍认可的重要历史人物，他的思想影响着人们的为人处世，对东亚地区及世界其他地区均有深远意义。

◎《圣迹图》中的孔子画像
明朝仇英绘

◎ 中国最大的孔庙
位于山东曲阜

故事

春秋时期，孔子是公认最博学的人之一，但其本人却非常谦逊，常常向他人请教。

一日，孔子来到鲁国太庙祭拜国君先祖。他一进太庙就向人问这问那，几乎每一件事都问到了。有人讥笑他说：“谁说圣人无所不知？他连祭祀的仪式都不知道。”

孔子答道：“对任何不甚了解的事情，我都会问个明白。正因如此，我才会懂得更多。”

几天后，孔子及其学生来到卫国。卫国有个大夫名孔圉。孔圉去世后，他被赐“文”的谥号，所以后来人们又尊称他为“孔文子”。

孔子的学生子贡却不认为孔圉配得上那样高贵的谥号。他问孔子：“孔圉有才，但卫国有比他更有才之人。况且，他在世时做过不少错事。为什么他被赐予如此高贵的谥号？”

孔子说：“因为他敏而好学，又不耻下问。”

文化链接

"子"和"诸子百家"

"子"加在姓之后，是中国古代对道德高尚、知识渊博或有较高社会地位之人的尊称，如孔子和老子。

孔子和老子所在的春秋时期（公元前770年—公元前476年）是中国哲学大发展的开端。"诸子百家"指的就是大量活跃在先秦时期的思想家及其学派，此现象史称"百家争鸣"。其中，影响最大的学派有儒家、法家、道家、墨家、阴阳家等。

《论语》

《论语》是一本记录孔子及其同时代思想家言论的著作，该书由孔子的弟子编写。《论语》是儒家经典之作，两千多年来，该书已成为全球最具影响力著作之一。

◎《论语》
韩国首尔成均馆大学博物馆藏品

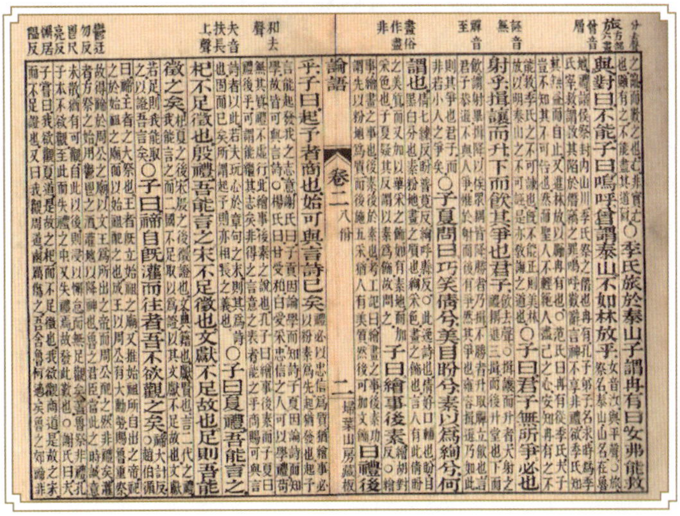

◎《论语》书页

◎ 孔子（中间靠左）、摩西（中）和梭伦（中间靠右）的雕像
美国联邦最高法院东入口上方的主雕像群

美国联邦最高法院建筑上的孔子雕像

在美国联邦最高法院东入口上方的中间位置，可以看到孔子和颁布《十诫》的摩西以及希腊立法者梭伦组成的雕像群。设计师想表达这样的想法：美国的法律体系来源于之前的文明，孔子、摩西以及梭伦分别代表了对美国法律制度发展有着深远影响的三种东方文明。

讨论

1. 故事中孔子是如何变得博学的？
2. 如果你有不理解的问题，你是否会羞于问他人，包括不如你的人？请给出理由。

III LEGENDARY PHYSICIAN BIAN QUE

Introduction

Bian Que (407 BC–310 BC), the earliest known Chinese physician, was the first to rely primarily on pulse taking and physical examination to diagnose diseases in the history of traditional Chinese medicine. According to *Records of the Grand Historian*, Bian Que's medical skills were so amazing that he could bring the dying back to life.

In China, there are more than ten Bian Que Temples commemorating the legendary physician.

◎ *Writing about Repairing Bian Que's Tomb*, inscribed on a Qing Dynasty tablet in Tangyin in Henan Province

Story Time

When Bian Que met with Duke Huan, Bian Que told the duke that he had a disease that was only skin deep but should be treated immediately. The duke replied that he was feeling very well and certainly not ill.

Ten days later, Bian Que saw the duke again and informed him that the disease had entered his muscles. The duke was rather annoyed, not uttering a word.

After another ten days, Bian Que told the duke that the disease was in the stomach and intestines, but he received the same response.

After ten more days, Bian Que again came to see the duke, but this time he said nothing and ran out of the room. The duke was puzzled, sending a messenger to find the reason. Bian Que replied, "When a disease is only skin deep, it can be treated with hot compresses; when in muscles with acupuncture; when in the stomach and intestines with heat-clearing medicine. However, when it penetrates the bone marrow, what can a doctor do? Now that the disease has spread into his bone marrow, it is meaningless for me to make further comments."

Just as Bian Que had predicted, the duke became ill five days later and died shortly after.

Bian Que Meeting with Duke Huan, painted at the Long Corridor of the Summer Palace in Beijing

Cultural Links

Traditional Chinese medicine

Traditional Chinese medicine (TCM) is based on various forms of Chinese medical practices throughout over 2,500 years, which includes herbal medicine, acupuncture, massage, breathing exercise, dietary therapy, and so on.

The concepts of the body and the disease in TCM place more emphasis on dynamic processes than material structure. While health is thought as the harmonious balance between the body and the outside world, the disease is considered imbalance in the interaction.

TCM diagnosis aims to trace symptoms to an underlying disharmony, by examining the tongue, skin, and eyes, listening for particular sounds, inquiring about the symptoms, the eating, sleeping habits and others, and feeling the pulse.

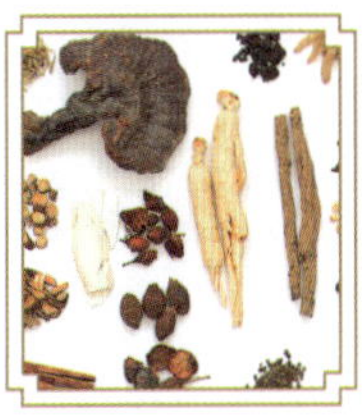

Herbal medicine

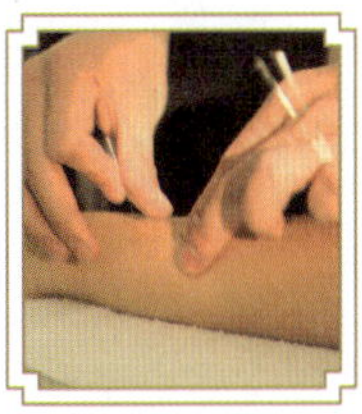

Acupuncture

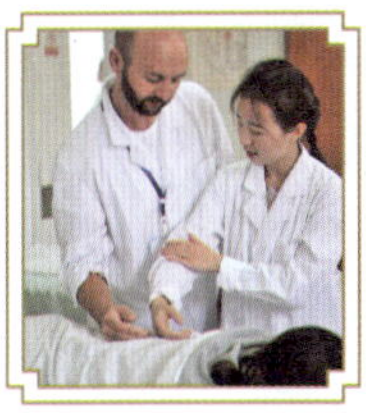

Massage

Breathing exercise

Dietary therapy

Concealing ailment and refusing treatment

This Chinese idiom derives from the story that Duke Huan ignores Bian Que's medical advice and finally dies of the disease. The idiom literally criticizes those who are ill but conceal their illness and refuse any medical treatment. It can also be used figuratively to criticize those who overlook their faults and reject advice from other people.

Ancient Greek medicine

The ancient Greek medicine can be represented by the Hippocratic School of Medicine, which was founded by Hippocrates (460 BC–370 BC), who is considered one of the most outstanding physicians in the history of medicine. The school proposes the well-known Humoralism: The human body is filled with four basic substances, called humors, which refer to blood, phlegm, yellow bile, and black bile. The four humors are in balance when a person is healthy. Diseases and disabilities result from improper balance of the four humors.

Discussion

1. How did Bian Que diagnose Duke Huan during the times he met with the duke?
2. Would you go to a hospital of traditional Chinese medicine when you are sick? State your reasons.

叁　神医扁鹊

引

扁鹊（公元前 407 年—公元前 310 年）是中国历史上第一位名医，奠定了中医学的切脉诊断方法，开启了中医学的先河。据《史记》记载，“天下尽以扁鹊为能生死人。”

在中国，有十余座扁鹊庙用以纪念这位神医。

◎《重修扁鹊先生墓文》
河南汤阴的清朝碑文

故事

扁鹊进见蔡桓公。扁鹊对蔡桓公说，他肌肤纹理间有些小毛病，不医治恐怕会加重。蔡桓公说他很好，没有病。

过了十天，扁鹊再次进见蔡桓公，告诉他说，他的病在肌肉里，不及时医治将会更加严重。蔡桓公面色不悦，一言不发。

又过了十天，扁鹊再一次进见蔡桓公，告诉他说，他的病在肠胃里了，不及时治疗将要更加严重。蔡桓公依然没有理睬扁鹊。

又过了十天，扁鹊进见蔡桓公，这次扁鹊什么也没说，而是掉头就跑。蔡桓公疑惑，于是派人询问。扁鹊说："小病在皮肤纹理之间，可以用汤熨治好；病在肌肉里面，用针灸可以治好；病在肠胃里，用火剂汤可以治好。但如果病在骨髓里，医生就没有办法医治了。现在病已深入骨髓，我再说也无用了。"

如扁鹊所见，过了五天，蔡桓公感到身体不适，不久就过世了。

《扁鹊见蔡桓公》
北京颐和园长廊画作

文化链接

中医

中医是基于中国各种行医治疗方法的医学，至今已有2500多年的历史。中医包括草药、针灸、按摩、气功、食疗等。

中医对于人体和疾病的观点反映出中医强调动态过程，而非物质结构。中医认为，人体与天地阴阳调和为健康，不和则产生疾病。

中医在诊疗时往往追根溯源，通过望、闻、问、切四种手段诊断疾病。

讳疾忌医

此成语出自蔡桓公不相信扁鹊的诊断最终因病而逝的故事，用于批评某些隐瞒疾病，不愿接受医治的人。该成语也可用来批评掩饰缺点，不愿接受他人意见的人。

草药

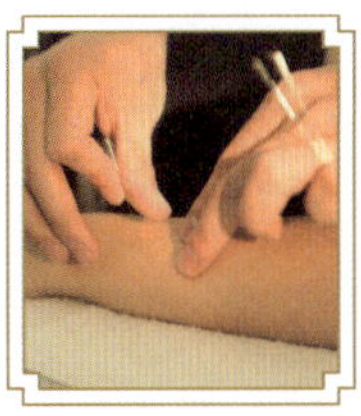

针灸

按摩

气功

食疗

古希腊医学

古希腊医学以希波克拉底学派为代表。该学派由古希腊名医希波克拉底（公元前460年—公元前370年）创建。希波克拉底是医学史上最著名的医生之一。该学派的主要观点为“体液学说”，他们认为机体的生命由四种体液决定：血、黏液、黄胆汁和黑胆汁。四体液平衡，则身体健康；四体液失调，则产生疾病。

讨论

1. 扁鹊见蔡桓公时如何诊断蔡桓公患有疾病？
2. 当身体不好时，你会去看中医吗？请说明理由。

IV MAO SUI RECOMMENDING HIMSELF

Introduction

Mao Sui (285BC-228BC) was a retainer of Lord Pingyuan in the Zhao State, unknown to public for three years. In 257 BC, he recommended himself as an envoy to the Chu State. With his outstanding courage and convincing argument, Mao Sui persuaded Chu to make an alliance with Zhao. Because of this, Mao Sui earned the reputation of "having a silver tongue to beat a mighty army."

◎ Guangfu Ancient City in Handan of Hebei Province, granted to Mao Sui as his fief in the Warring States Period

Story Time

During the Warring States Period, when the army of Qin surrounded Handan, the capital of the Zhao State, Lord Pingyuan was under order to seek aid from the Chu State by forging an alliance with it. Thus, he decided to visit the Chu State, bringing twenty retainers with him.

Just then, one of the retainers, Mao Sui, came forward and recommended himself, "My name is Mao Sui. I hear you are going to Chu for the alliance. My lord, sincerely hope you can take me along."

"How long have you been here?" Lord Pingyuan asked.

"Three years."

"It's been quite a while ... An able man can quickly show his talent just like an awl in a bag with its point always sticking out. You have been here for three years, unknown to me yet. Let me get this straight, you can hardly have any talent! Since it is going to be our toughest mission, I am afraid I can't take along a useless man."

Hearing this, Mao Sui responded with confidence, "What I am asking for right now is to be put in the bag. Had I been put there earlier, the awl would thrust outright instead of showing its tip only."

Lord Pingyuan finally agreed to take him along to Chu.

Cultural Links

Four Lords of the Warring States

Succeeding the chaotic Spring and Autumn Period and preceding the Qin Dynasty, the Warring States Period (the 5th century BC–221 BC) is an era of intensive warfare and revolution.

The Four Lords of the late Warring States Period were four political activists in their respective states, including Wei Wuji (Lord Xinling of Wei), Huang Xie (Lord Chunshen of Chu), Tian Wen (Lord Mengchang of Qi) and Zhao Sheng (Lord Pingyuan of Zhao). All four are renowned for being courteous to the scholars. With great military power and wealth, they housed many talented retainers to deal with political opponents internally while to fight against enemy states externally.

◎ An Eastern Han Dynasty brick showing the scene of salvaging the Ding, held by the Henan Museum in Zhengzhou in Henan Province

The Nine Dings

The Nine Dings are said to be a collection of ancient Chinese dings cast by Yu the Great, each with the carvings of scenery and marvels in one of the Nine Provinces. In different dynasties, they all were regarded as the

◎ *The Nine Dings* in the Warring States Period, held by the Hebei Museum in Shijiazhuang in Hebei Province

symbol of national political power and later as a national treasure.

Lord Pingyuan praised Mao Sui for significantly raising the national prestige, which outweighed Nine Dings.

Another example is a Chinese idiom "One word is as heavy as the Nine Dings", which means his words play a decisive role or he is a trustworthy man who never breaks his promise.

Application Essay

Self-recommendation is very important in western culture. For example, students who want to attend college need to write an application essay. They have to state their characters, personal experience and strengths to show that they have the qualification and are the right ones to be chosen.

Discussion

1. Why do you think Mao Sui could succeed in recommending himself to Lord Pingyuan?
2. How would you introduce yourself in an interview?

肆　毛遂自荐

引

毛遂是赵国平原君门客，三年寂寂无闻。公元前257年，他自荐出使楚国。凭着过人胆识和雄辩伟才，毛遂说服楚国与赵合纵，由此获得“三寸之舌，强于百万之师”的美誉。

◎ 河北邯郸的广府古城
战国时期授为毛遂封地

故事

战国时期，赵国首都邯郸被秦军围困，平原君奉命向楚国寻求外援，意图与其合纵抵抗秦国。于是，他决定带上二十个门客一起前往楚国。

此时，一个叫毛遂的门客上前说道，“我叫毛遂，听说您要去楚国劝其合纵，我诚愿随您前往！”

平原君问道，“你来我这多久了？”

“三年。”

“那时间可不短了……一个有才能的人，就好比装在囊中的锥子，它的尖总能显露出来。可你在我府上三年，我连名字都没听过。请恕我直言，你恐怕没什么才干吧！这次前往，身负重任，恐怕不能带上无用之人。”

听闻此言，毛遂胸有成竹地回应道：“我现在就是请求您把我放到囊中。如果我早被放入囊中，肯定早就脱颖而出了，怎会只是冒出一点尖呐！”

平原君最终接受了毛遂的自荐，带他一同前往楚国。

文化链接

战国四公子

战国（公元前 5 世纪—公元前 221 年）上承春秋乱世，下启大秦帝国，是战争和变革并存的风云时代。

战国四公子指战国末期四位有名的政治活动家：魏国的信陵君魏无忌、楚国的春申君黄歇、齐国的孟尝君田文、赵国的平原君赵胜。四位以礼贤下士而知名，他们拥有强大的兵力和财力，收养了众多门客，对内对付政敌，对外抗争敌国。

◎ 东汉“泗水捞鼎”画像砖
河南郑州的河南博物院展品

九鼎

九鼎，据传由大禹铸成，每个鼎身分别镌刻有九州之一的景致和奇迹。九鼎在不同朝代都是王权至高无上的象征，后奉为“国宝”。

◎ 战国时期的“九鼎”
河北石家庄的河北博物馆藏品

平原君曾夸赞毛遂：因为毛遂，赵国地位重过九鼎。

还有一个例子是中国成语“一言九鼎”，指一个人说话分量大，起决定作用；或褒赞他是个一诺千金之人。

申请书

自荐在西方文化里非常重要。例如，学生在申请大学时，必须要写自荐文书。在自荐文书中，需要陈述自己的独特之处、个人经历、自己的优势，来说明有资格申请该校、适合该校。

讨论

1. 你觉得毛遂为什么可以成功地向平原君自荐？
2. 在面试现场，你如何向面试官推荐自己？

V XIANG YU CUTTING OFF ALL HIS MEANS OF RETREAT

Introduction

Xiang Yu (232 BC–202 BC) was a prominent general in the late Qin Dynasty. He is commonly known by his self-styled title of Overlord of Western Chu.

The poem *A Quatrain* written by Li Qingzhao (1084–c.1155) portrays Xiang Yu's heroism:

A Quatrain

Be man of men while you're alive,
And soul of souls if you were dead.
Think of Xiang Yu who'd not survive,
His men whose blood for him was shed.

(Translated by Xu Yuanchong)

⊙ The bronze statue of Xiang Yu proclaiming himself the *Overlord of Western Chu*, standing in Suqian in Jiangsu Province

Xiang Yu Cutting Off All His Means of Retreat, inscribed on the wall of the Yuexiu Park in Guangzhou in Guangdong Province

Story Time

In 208 BC, the city of Julu was surrounded by Qin troops for nearly a month. In order to relieve the city, the Chu State sent 50,000 soldiers led by Xiang Yu and Song Yi to fight against the Qin army.

When the Chu army advanced towards Julu, Xiang Yu sent 20,000 soldiers to cross the river first and attack the Qin army, but they were unable to raise the siege. Some soldiers were frustrated, not willing to fight against the Qin army any more. Knowing that determination and morale were the key to victory, Xiang Yu was lost in thought.

The next day, he made a life-and-death decision: sending his entire force into the battle. After crossing the river, Xiang Yu ordered the troops to sink all the boats and smash all the cooking pots after a three-day supply was prepared. The soldiers realized that their way back was cut off, and they had no choice but to win the battle. If they failed, they could not survive.

Soon the two armies fought. Although having far smaller forces, the brave and fearless Chu army eventually scored a great victory after nine engagements, defeating the Qin army of 300,000 soldiers. This battle is known as the Battle of Julu in China's history. After the battle, the Qin Dynasty began to lose power and shortly came to an end.

Cultural Links

The Qin army

The Qin Dynasty (221 BC–207 BC), founded by Qin Shi Huang as the first feudal dynasty of Imperial China, was one of the world's strongest military powers supported by a stable economy.

In the Battle of Julu, the Qin army had 300,000 soldiers, six times that of the Chu army. Meanwhile, they were well armed with bronze swords, crossbows, arrowheads, etc. according to the Terracotta Army in Shaanxi province excavated in 1974. These were the most advanced weapons of the time in the world.

In spite of having far larger forces and more powerful weapons, the Qin army lost the Battle of Julu mainly due to poor military strategy and management with serious infighting.

The Art of War

The strategy of cutting off all means of retreat is also mentioned in the book *The Art of War*, which, written by Sun Tzu and translated in English by Lionel Giles, says, "A skilful general carries his men deep into hostile territory before he shows his hand. He burns his boats and breaks his cooking-pots; like a shepherd driving a flock of sheep, he drives his men this way and that, and nothing shows where he is going."

The Art of War is an ancient Chinese military treatise dating from the Spring and Autumn Period and remains highly influential in modern warfare. Over the past two decades, people all over the world have been adapting the strategies in the book and applying them to politics, business, and others.

Julius Caesar crossing the Rubicon

In January of 49 BC, Caesar brought his army across the river to fight against Rome, which sparked the Roman Civil War and ultimately led to Caesar's becoming dictator for life. As his army marched through the shallow river, he said, "The dice is cast."

Therefore, the idiom "crossing the Rubicon" in English means to pass a point of no return.

⊙ Bronze swords

⊙ A crossbow

⊙ Arrowheads

Discussion

1. With far smaller forces, why do you think the Chu army managed to win the Battle of Julu?
2. Would you cross the Rubicon if you had to perform an extremely difficult task?

伍　项羽破釜沉舟

引

项羽（公元前 232 年—公元前 202 年）是秦末的著名将领。他自立西楚霸王的故事在民间代代相传。

宋代诗人李清照（1084 年—约 1155 年）在《夏日绝句》中曾描述了项羽的英雄事迹。

《夏日绝句》

生当作人杰，死亦为鬼雄。

至今思项羽，不肯过江东。

◎ 项羽自封“西楚霸王”场景
江苏宿迁的青铜雕塑

◎ 项羽破釜沉舟
广东广州越秀公园内壁雕

故事

公元前 208 年，秦军包围巨鹿城近一个月。楚国以项羽和宋义为帅，发兵 5 万，解救巨鹿。

不久，楚军已行近巨鹿。项羽派两万楚兵先行渡河进攻秦军，然收效甚微。此时，一些士兵士气低落，甚至出现厌战情绪。项羽深知取胜的关键在于军队意志坚定、斗志高昂。于是，他陷入了沉思。

第二天，他做出了一个生死抉择：孤注一掷，率领全部兵马渡河作战。渡河后，项羽下令将全部行军做饭的锅砸碎，又下令将渡船全部砸沉，只准士卒每人带足三日口粮。士卒眼见无路可退，意识到此役若不能胜则难以存活。

不久楚军与秦军展开交锋。尽管双方兵力悬殊，但无所畏惧的楚军无不奋勇搏杀。经过九次恶战，楚军大败秦军 30 万，巨鹿大捷。此役史称“巨鹿之战”。经此一役，秦朝一蹶不振，很快覆灭。

文化链接

秦军

秦朝（公元前 221 年—公元前 207 年）是中国第一个封建王朝，其开国皇帝为秦始皇。秦朝是当时世界上军事实力最强大的国家之一，一直都有稳定的经济后盾支撑。

巨鹿之战，秦军拥兵 30 万，是楚军的六倍。同时，秦军装备精良。从 1974 年陕西省出土的兵马俑文物中可以发现，当时秦军使用青铜剑、弓弩、箭头等武器，这些都是当时世界上最先进的武器。

秦军兵力与装备远胜楚军，但由于战略失当、管理混乱，秦军最终输掉了巨鹿之战。

《孙子兵法》

破釜沉舟的策略在《孙子兵法》一书中也有提及。该书由孙武所著，翟林奈·贾尔斯将其译为英语。书中说道："帅与之深入诸侯之地，而发其机，焚舟破釜，若驱群羊，驱而往，驱而来，莫知所之。"

《孙子兵法》为中国春秋时期兵法专著，其内容对于现代战争仍有较大影响。近二十年来，世界各国还在研究该书在政治、商业等领域的应用。

凯撒穿越卢比孔河

公元前 49 年 1 月，凯撒率军穿越卢比孔河与罗马军队交战。这一事件被认为是罗马内战的导火索。最终，凯撒获得了胜利并成为罗马帝国终身独裁官。凯撒军队穿越卢比孔河时，凯撒说："骰子已经掷下。"

因此，英语中"穿越卢比孔河"这一习语用来表示破釜沉舟，没有退路。

◎ 青铜剑

◎ 箭弩

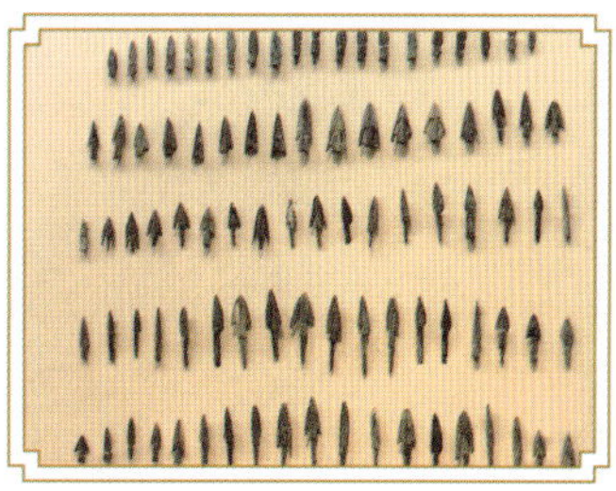

◎ 箭头

讨论

1. 为什么楚军能在兵力悬殊的情况下赢得巨鹿之战?

2. 你在完成一项非常艰难的任务时是否会破釜沉舟?

VI CAI LUN INVENTING PAPER

Introduction

Cai Lun (?–121 AD) was an official and inventor of the Han Dynasty. Traditionally, it is believed that he invented the paper along with the papermaking process. As one of the Four Great Inventions of ancient China, papermaking greatly encouraged the civilizational development in China and other countries worldwide.

In the book *The 100: A Ranking of the Most Influential Persons in History* written by American writer Michael H. Hart, Cai Lun is ranked as the seventh most influential person in history, even above Einstein, Galileo, Aristotle, and others.

◎ The papermaking process, invented by Cai Lun in the Han Dynasty

◎ The statue showing the scene of Cai Lun inventing paper, standing in the National Museum of Chinese Writing in Anyang in Henan Province

Story Time

Cai Lun began to serve in the imperial court from 75 AD. In 89 AD, he was promoted with the title of *Shangfang Ling*, an officer in charge of manufacturing instruments and weapons.

At that time, writings and inscriptions were generally made on tablets of bamboo or pieces of silk. As the silk was costly and the bamboo was heavy, neither of them was convenient to use. Thus, Cai Lun decided to find a writing medium that was cheaper and lighter.

Then, he kept on looking for new materials, while making no progress at all for weeks. One day, he saw an old man stripping tree barks. He touched the inner barks, which felt perfectly smooth. Immediately, he tried writing on them, excited to find that they were easy to write on.

Just a few days later, however, the characters on the tree barks became illegible as the barks turned dry and wrinkled. Cai Lun was rather disappointed, but more determined. After hundreds of experiments, he finally invented the paper that was made from the bark of trees, remnants of hemp, rags of cloth and fishing nets, which was cheap, light, smooth, and preservable.

Cai Lun then submitted his invention to Emperor An of Han, who was extremely pleased with it and granted Cai Lun the Marquis of Longting in 114 AD. From that time, people in China began to use paper.

Papermaking

Compass

Gunpowder

Printing

Cultural Links

Paper of Marquis Cai

In 114 AD, Emperor An of Han promoted Cai Lun to the Marquis of Longting because of his outstanding contribution to papermaking. As a result, the paper invented by Cai Lun was called the Paper of Marquis Cai.

Besides the Paper of Marquis Cai, many advancements in the Han Dynasty (206 BC–220 AD) made it a golden age in China's history, such as the invention of the armillary sphere and the earthquake weathervane, the first use of negative numbers, the application of anaesthesia, etc. Nowadays, the ethnic group with the largest population in China refers to themselves as the "Han people" and the Chinese script is referred to as "Han characters."

Four Great Inventions of ancient China

Four Great Inventions of ancient China are inventions from ancient China that are celebrated in Chinese culture for their historical significance and as symbols of ancient China's advanced science and technology.

These great inventions refer to papermaking, compass, gunpowder, and printing. These four inventions had a large impact on the development of the civilization of China and the other parts of the world.

Papyrus

Papyrus is a material similar to thick paper that was used by ancient Egyptians as a writing medium in the 3rd century BC. Different from the writing medium recognizable as paper in modern times, which was invented by Cai Lun, papyrus was made from the pith of the papyrus plant, heavy, coarse, and hard to make.

⊙ Papyrus Letter dated 5 May 257 BC, held by the British Museum in London, the United Kingdom

Discussion

1. What are the characteristics of the Paper of Marquis Cai?
2. Which do you prefer, paper books or electronic books? State your reasons.

陆　蔡伦造纸

引

蔡伦（？—公元 121 年）是汉朝时期的朝臣和发明家。据传，他是造纸术的发明者。这项发明被列入中国四大发明，极大地促进了中国文明和世界文明的发展。

美国作家麦克·哈特在《影响人类历史进程的 100 名人排行榜》一书中将蔡伦排在第七位，甚至排在爱因斯坦、伽利略、亚里士多德等人前面。

◎ 造纸术
由汉朝蔡伦发明

◎ 蔡伦造纸场景
河南安阳中国文字博物馆内雕塑

故事

蔡伦于公元 75 年入宫，并于公元 89 年升为尚方令，掌管皇宫工具和武器制造。

那时，人们在竹片上书写篆刻，也在丝绸上写字。但竹片沉重，丝绸昂贵，两者皆不宜用于书写。因此，蔡伦决定寻找一种轻便廉价的书写介质。

此后几周，蔡伦一直忙于寻找新的书写材质，却毫无进展。一日，他见一位老者正用刀削树皮，就摸了摸树皮内侧，手感光滑无比。他马上试着在树皮上写字，惊喜地发现树皮竟如此易于书写。

然而几天后，树皮开始干皱，字迹也越来越难以辨认。蔡伦虽略感失望，却更坚定了寻找新材质的想法。经过数百次试验，他终于用树皮、麻头、破布、鱼网做成了纸。这种纸造价低廉，纸质轻便，书写流畅，易于保存。

之后，蔡伦将其发明呈献汉安帝。汉安帝龙颜大悦，于公元 114 年册封蔡伦为“龙亭侯”。从此，纸开始在中国使用。

造纸术

指南针

火药

印刷术

文化链接

蔡侯纸

因蔡伦造纸有功，汉安帝于公元 114 年册封蔡伦为“蔡亭侯”。因而，人们将蔡伦发明的纸称为“蔡侯纸”。

除了蔡侯纸的发明，汉朝（公元前 206 年—公元 220 年）很多方面的发展使之成为中国历史上的黄金时代，如发明浑天仪和地动仪、首次使用负数和应用麻药等。至今，中国人口最多的民族被称为“汉族”，中国文字被称为“汉字”。

中国四大发明

中国四大发明是中国文化和中国古代科学技术的象征，有着极其重要的历史地位。

中国四大发明指：造纸术、指南针、火药及印刷术。这四大发明对中国及世界文明的发展产生了极其重要的影响。

莎草纸

莎草纸是古埃及人在公元前 3 世纪开始使用的书写材料，材质类似于厚纸。与蔡伦发明的现代意义上的纸不同，莎草纸由一种叫纸莎草植物的茎制成，其纸质厚重、纸面粗糙、制造复杂。

◎ 日期为公元前257年5月5日的莎草纸信件
英国伦敦大英博物馆藏品

讨论

1. 蔡侯纸有什么特点？
2. 你更喜欢纸质书还是电子书？请说明原因。

VII KONG RONG YIELDING BIGGER PEARS

Introduction

Kong Rong (153 AD–208 AD) was a man of the 20th generation descendant of Confucius. In the *Three-Character Classic*, one of the texts used for traditional elementary education, his story of yielding bigger pears is mentioned with twelve Chinese characters. The four three-character verses are as follows:

(róng sì suì)	Rong, at the age of four,
(néng ràng lí)	could yield the (bigger) pears.
(tì yú zhăng)	To respect and love the elders,
(yí xiān zhī)	is one of the first things to know.

◎ The portrait of Kong Rong from the *Portraits of Famed Ministers*, compiled during the reign of Emperor Qian Long of the Qing Dynasty

Story Time

In 153 AD of the Eastern Han Dynasty in China's history, Kong Rong was born in the Lu State (present Qufu of Shandong province). As a descendent of Confucius, he was educated to be courteous from childhood.

When Kong Rong was four years old, one day, his father came home with some pears. Kong Rong and his brothers leapt with joy, coming over to stand around their father, and looked at all the pears on the table. They found that the pears seemed great but different in size.

His father picked up a pear, which happened to be the biggest one, and gave it to Kong Rong affectionately. Kong Rong shook his head and handed the pear over to his eldest brother. Then, he picked out the smallest one for himself.

Seeing Kong Rong's behavior, his father felt delighted and asked, "Why did you choose the smallest one?" Kong Rong answered, "I am younger, so I should eat the smaller pear and leave the bigger ones to my elder brothers." Hearing this, his father nodded approvingly with a smile.

When growing up, Kong Rong became a well-known Confucian scholar. His morals and words produced a great influence at that time and afterwards.

◎ A set of two stamps: *Kong Rong Yielding Bigger Pears*, issued by China Post
Left: T-1 *Sharing the Pears*
Right: T-2 *Yielding Bigger Pears*

Cultural Links

Three-Character Classic

The *Three-Character Classic* was probably written in the 13th century during the Song Dynasty. With the simple three-character verses, young children were able to learn many common characters, grammar structures, China's history and the basis of Confucian morality.

The *Three-Character Classic* is usually among the articles used in a traditional ceremony of the One-Year-Old Catch (Draw Lots). On the day when a child is one year old, he is asked to catch his favorite article without any instructions or implications. According to the custom, he who catches the *Three-Character Classic* will be interested in reading and become a scholar in the future.

The first four verses in the *Three-Character Classic* state the core of Confucianism.

(rén zhī chū)	People at birth
(xìng běn shàn)	are naturally good (kind-hearted).
(xìng xiāng jìn)	Their natures are similar
(xí xiāng yuǎn)	but their habits make them different (from each other).

⊙ The items, including the *Three-Character Classic*, used in the ceremony of One-Year-Old Catch, displayed at the Capital Museum in Beijing

Idioms related to Kong Rong

1) The best of friends in spite of the difference of ages

According to the *History of the Later Han*, Kong Rong and Mi Heng made good friends in spite of the fact that the former was forty while the latter being about twenty. When asked whom he would consider talented, Mi Heng replied, "First, there is Kong Rong." Kong Rong also thought highly of Mi Heng so he recommended him to Cao Cao. This idiom later refers to the deep friendship between those with a huge age gap.

2) How could there be unbroken eggs under a toppled nest?

In 208 AD, Kong Rong was put to death by Cao Cao. When he was arrested, his children were playing chess. Others urged them to escape but got the answer, "How could there be unbroken eggs under a toppled nest?" This later was used to describe that when a group suffers, all individuals in it will be affected.

Traditional courtesy in the West: Ladis First

To respect and love the elders is one of the basics in Chinese traditional culture. In the West, Ladis First is considered a social rule in traditional courtesy.

Following the rule of Lady First, the gentlemen should respect, help, protect and take good care of ladies. For example, he should open the door for a lady, help her to have her coat, assist her with her chair when she stands up or sits down, offer his seat in a crowded train or bus, and so on.

Discussion

1. What do you think of Kong Rong's courtesy in the story?
2. Will you take the courtesy seat, if one is available, on public occasions? Why or why not?

柒 孔融让梨

引

孔融（公元 153 年—公元 208 年）是孔子的二十世孙。他让梨的故事在中国传统启蒙教材《三字经》中被提及，共十二字。这四句三字经是：

融四岁，——孔融四岁时，

能让梨。——就知道把大的梨让给兄长吃。

弟于长，——这种尊爱兄长的道理（“弟”通“悌”，表示“尊爱”），

宜先知。——是每个人首先应该知道的。

◎《历代名臣像解》中的孔融像
清朝乾隆年间汇编

故事

公元 153 年，中国东汉时期，孔融在鲁国（今山东曲阜）出生。作为孔子的后代，他从小就被教育要谦卑礼让。

孔融四岁时，有一天，父亲带了一些梨回家。兄弟们雀跃着围住了父亲，看着桌上的梨。梨看上去都很不错，但个头有大有小。

父亲拿起了其中最大的一个梨，亲切地递给了孔融。小孔融摇头不要，把大梨递给了长兄。然后，自己选了一个最小的梨。

看到孔融把大的梨给了兄长，父亲心中很是欢喜，问道：“为什么你选了个最小的呢？”孔融说：“我年纪小，应该吃小梨，大的留给哥哥们吃。”父亲听后笑着频频点头。

长大后，孔融成为一代名儒，他的品格与言论对当时和后世产生了很大影响。

◎ 中国邮政发行的一套两枚邮票：《孔融让梨》
左：T-1《分果》
右：T-2《让梨》

文化链接

《三字经》

《三字经》很可能写于 13 世纪宋朝时期。通过浅显的三字一句，孩子们可以学习许多常用字、语法结构、中国历史和儒家思想。

在传统的“抓周”仪式中，所用的物品常包括《三字经》。孩子一岁时，家人会在没有任何指导和暗示的情况下，让他抓取一件最喜欢的物品。根据风俗，抓到《三字经》的孩子以后会喜欢读书并成为学者。

《三字经》开头的四句表达了儒家的核心思想：人之初，性本善。性相近，习相远 。

◎ “抓周”仪式用品（包括《三字经》）
北京首都博物馆展品

与孔融有关的成语

1）忘年之交

据《后汉书》记载：“衡始弱冠，而融年四十，遂与为交友。”当有人问祢衡认为谁是才子时，他回答说孔融是第一才子。孔融也很钦佩祢衡，因此将其推荐给了曹操。这句成语后来指年辈不相当而结交为友。

2）覆巢之下，安有完卵？

公元208年，孔融被曹操处死。当他被抓时，他的孩子们正在下棋。其他人催他们赶快逃跑，而他们回答：“覆巢之下，安有完卵？”这句话后来被用作表示当整体遭殃时，组成整体的所有个体也会受到影响。

西方礼让传统：女士优先

在中国，尊爱长辈是基本的传统文化；而在西方，女士优先是礼让传统中的社交规则。

根据女士优先的规则，男士应该尊重、帮助、保护和照顾女士。比如，男士应该为女士开门，帮助拿取外套，在其起立或落座时帮助拉椅子，在拥挤的车上让座等。

讨论

1. 对故事中孔融的礼让，你怎么看？
2. 如果公众场合有爱心专座，你会坐吗？为什么？

VIII THREE VISITS TO THE THATCHED COTTAGE

Introduction

The story of *Three Visits to the Thatched Cottage* is collected in the book *Records of the Three Kingdoms*, written by Chen Shou.

According to the story, Zhuge Liang (181 AD–234 AD), one of the greatest statesmen and military strategists in ancient China, had lived in a thatched cottage before Liu Bei (161 AD–223 AD), the founder of the Shu-Han State, paid "three visits to the thatched cottage" to invite Zhuge Liang to follow him.

◎ The *Painting of Three Visits to the Thatched Cottage* by Dai Jin of the Ming Dynasty, held by the Palace Museum in Beijing

◎ The statue of Zhuge Liang presenting *Longzhong Plan* for reunifying China to Liu Bei, standing at the Baidi Temple in Fengjie in Chongqing

Story Time

While Liu Bei was taking shelter under Liu Biao, the governor of Jing Province, Xu Shu, an advisor of Liu, recommended Zhuge Liang to him. When Xu was asked to invite Zhuge to meet Liu, he replied, "You must visit this man in person. He won't come to meet you."

The next day, bringing lots of gifts and accompanied by Guan Yu and Zhang Fei, Liu's blood brothers, he arrived at Zhuge Liang's house, a thatched cottage, where a servant told them that his master was not at home, so they had to leave.

Several days later in that winter, Liu Bei brought his blood brothers along with him to visit Zhuge Liang again. When they arrived, they saw a young man reading, who turned out to be Zhuge Liang's younger brother. He told them that Zhuge Liang was not at home, otherwise engaged. Then Liu asked the servant to pass a message to Zhuge Liang that Liu had come to visit him.

When the spring came the next year, Liu Bei decided to visit Zhuge Liang once again, much to the annoyance of his blood brothers. This time, Zhuge Liang was at home, but was asleep. Liu waited patiently until Zhuge Liang woke up. Affected by his three visits, Zhuge Liang presented to him a strategic plan to reunify China, also known as Longzhong Plan in China's history, and agreed to leave home and serve Liu as his strategist.

Cultural Links

The *Romance of the Three Kingdoms*

The *Romance of the Three Kingdoms* is a historical novel written by Luo Guanzhong. It is set in the turbulent years between the end of the Han dynasty and the Three Kingdoms Period (220 AD–280 AD) in China's history.

The three kingdoms refer to the states of Wei (founded in 220 AD by Cao Pi), Shu-Han (founded in 221 AD by Liu Bei), and Wu (founded in 229 AD by Sun Quan).

The book is acclaimed as one of the greatest classical novels of Chinese literature and of the most beloved works of literature in East Asia, and its literary influence in the region has been compared to that of the works of Shakespeare on English literature.

Quotes from Zhuge Liang

The wise win before they fight, while the ignorant fight to win.

Those who are skilled in combat do not become angered; those who are skilled at winning do not become afraid.

Good generals select intelligent officers, thoughtful advisors, and brave subordinates.

Wisdom from great minds

Great vision without great people is irrelevant. — Jim Collins

Never hire someone who knows less than you do about what he is hired to do.
— Malcolm Forbes

You can have the best strategy and the best building in the world, but if you don't have the hearts and minds of the people who work with you, none of it comes to life.
— Renee West

Discussion

1. Why did Zhuge Liang decide to follow Liu Bei?
2. If you were to build a team for a particular project, how would you invite people to join you?

捌　三顾茅庐

引

陈寿在其《三国志》一书中记载了三顾茅庐的故事。

据书中说，诸葛亮（公元 181 年—公元 234 年）被认为是中国古代最伟大的政治家和军事家之一，曾居于茅庐之中。刘备（公元 161 年—公元 223 年），蜀汉开国皇帝，曾三顾茅庐，力邀诸葛亮辅佐。

⊙ 明朝画家戴进所绘《三顾草庐图》北京故宫博物院展品

◎ 诸葛亮为刘备献上《隆中对》
重庆奉节白帝庙的雕塑

故事

刘备投靠荆州牧刘表时，手下谋士徐庶向刘备推荐诸葛亮。刘备让徐庶请诸葛亮来见他，但徐庶说：“这个人是不会来见你的，你要亲自去请他来。”

第二天，刘备备下厚礼，在结义兄弟关羽和张飞的陪同下来到诸葛亮的住处，发现诸葛亮的住所只是一间普通的茅庐。一个书童上前告诉他们诸葛亮已外出。他们只好回去。

还是那年冬天，几日后，刘备一行人再次拜访诸葛亮。进门时，见一青年正在读书。上前询问后才知道这个青年是诸葛亮的弟弟。他告诉刘备等人诸葛亮有事外出。于是刘备让一个书童代为传信，说刘备来访。

冬去春来。尽管刘备的两位结拜兄弟对拜访诸葛亮一事大为不满，刘备还是打算再去拜访诸葛亮。他们来到诸葛亮住所时，诸葛亮正在睡觉。刘备一行人就在屋外静静等候，直至诸葛亮醒来。刘备三次拜访的诚意打动了诸葛亮。于是，诸葛亮向刘备提出了自己平定天下的谋略（史称“隆中对”），并答应出山辅佐刘备。

文化链接

《三国演义》

《三国演义》是一部由罗贯中著写的历史小说。其背景为中国汉末到三国这一动荡的历史时期（公元 220 年—公元 280 年）。

三国指魏（公元 220 年由曹丕建立）、蜀（公元 221 年由刘备建立）与吴（公元 229 年由孙权建立）三个政权。

《三国演义》被誉为中国最好的古典小说之一，也是东亚地区最受欢迎的文学作品之一。该书在东亚地区的影响力可与莎士比亚作品在英语文学中地位相媲美。

诸葛亮语录

智者先胜而后求战，暗者先战而后求胜。

善战者不怒，善胜者不惧。

善将者，必有博闻多智者为腹心，沉审谨密者为耳目，勇悍善敌者为爪牙。

来自大师们的智慧

如果没有能干的员工，再宏伟的憧憬也只能是憧憬。——吉姆·柯林斯

永远不要招聘那些对其工作所知还不如你的人。——马尔科姆·福布斯

你可以有全世界最精妙的策略、最豪华的大楼，但如果你没有赢得员工的心，这一切都毫无意义。——雷妮·韦斯特

讨论

1. 为什么诸葛亮决定追随刘备？
2. 如果你要组建团队完成某一项目，你会如何邀请他人加入你的团队？

IX WANG XIZHI BEING FOND OF GEESE

Introduction

Wang Xizhi (303 AD–361 AD), living in the Wei and Jin Dynasties, was generally regarded as the greatest calligrapher in history. He had a mastery of all forms of Chinese calligraphy, especially of cursive script.

A Chinese character *goose* was inscribed on a stone tablet in the Guoqing Temple located at Mount Tiantai, Zhejiang Province. The character is unique in that it comprises of only one smooth stroke. However, only half of the one-stroke character was the original of Wang Xizhi, the other half being supplemented by Cao Lun, who spent seven years studying and copying Wang's calligraphy and eventually completed the remaining half with perfect coherency.

⊙ The tablet of one-stroke Chinese character *goose*, standing at the Guoqing Temple at Mount Tiantai in Zhejiang Province

Story Time

Wang Xizhi, known as the Sage of Calligraphy, was extremely fond of geese.

Once, when he learned that an old woman raised a lovable goose, he immediately sent for his servant to purchase it, only to be rejected by the old woman. He was a bit depressed and decided to see the charming goose with a few friends.

Hearing that the distinguished guest would come, the old woman felt very flattered and decided to treat the guest to a feast. When Wang arrived, he was heart-broken to find that the goose was on the plate, he sighed all day long without saying a word.

Another story was about a Daoist who was longing for a copy of hand-written *Daodejing* by Wang Xizhi.

Realizing the difficulty of obtaining the copy from a well-reputed calligrapher, the Daoist worked out his own "trick." He raised a flock of white geese and frequently walked them near the places where Wang often went outing with his friends.

Finally, the day came when the calligrapher came across the geese "by chance." Wang Xizhi was so attracted by those elegant creatures that he offered to buy them at once. Slowly, the Daoist replied, "Sorry, I won't sell my geese. But I might consider giving them to you if you are willing to write a copy of *Dao De Jing* for me."

Without any hesitation, Wang wrote a copy of the classic and returned with the flock of geese joyfully.

⊙ Part of *Wang Xizhi Watching the Geese* by Qian Xuan of the Yuan Dynasty, held by the Metropolitan Museum of Art in New York, the United States

Cultural Links

Men of letters in ancient China and their favorites

Many men of letters in ancient China showed special fondness of something, expressing both their enjoyment of life and their philosophies as well.

On a blue-and-white porcelain vase unearthed in 2006 were painted four pictures, which are Wang Xizhi Loving Orchids, Tao Yuanming Loving Chrysanthemums, Zhou Dunyi Loving Lotus Flowers and Lin Hejing Loving Winter-Sweets and Cranes. Hence, the group of pictures was given the name *Four Loves*.

⊙ The *Four Loves* on a blue-and-white porcelain vase, held by the Hubei Museum in Wuhan in Hubei Province

Styles of Chinese Calligraphy

There are five main styles of Chinese traditional calligraphy, which are seal, clerical, regular, semi-cursive and cursive styles. Ouyang Xun, Yan Zhenqing, Liu Gongquan and Zhao Mengfu are known as the Four Great Masters of Regular Style.

⊙ Seal Style

⊙ Clerical Style

⊙ Regular Style

⊙ Semi-Cursive Style

⊙ Cursive Style

◎ Ou Style

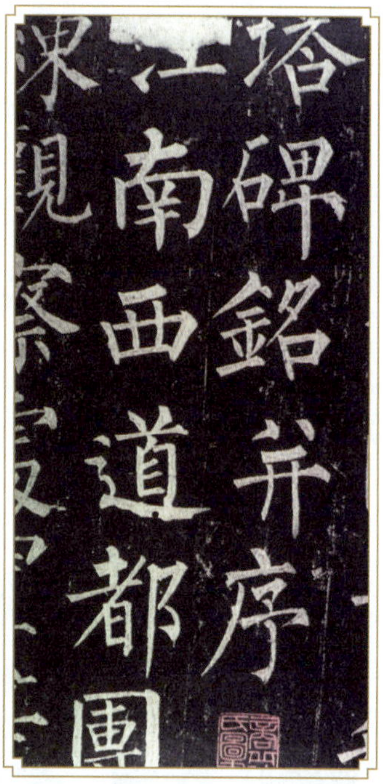

◎ Liu Style

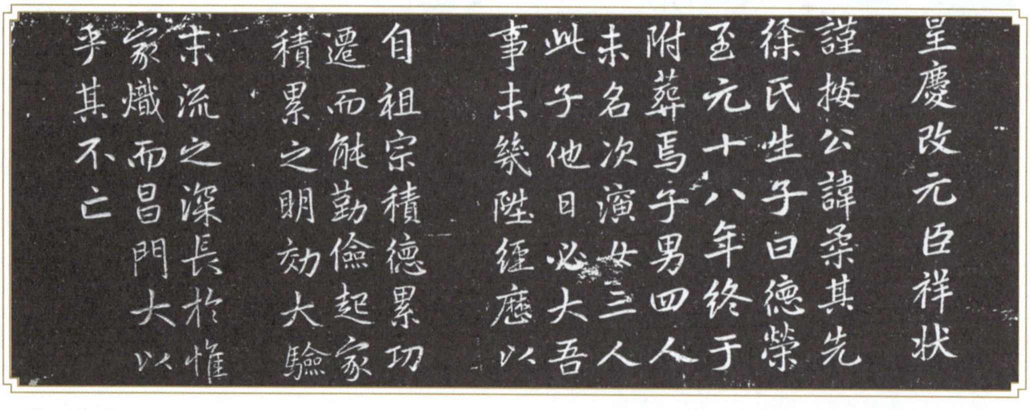

◎ Zhao Style

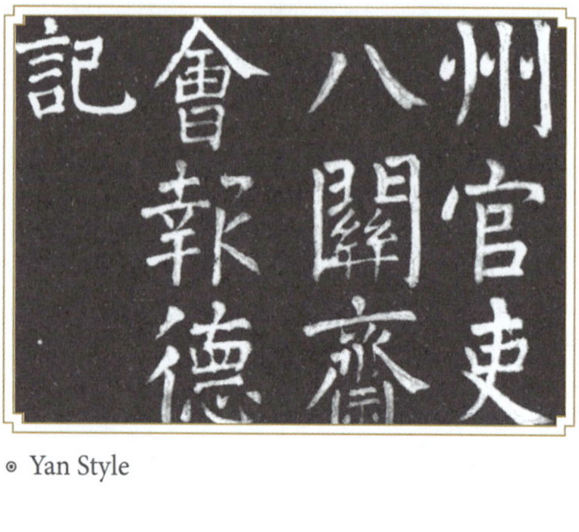

◎ Yan Style

Four Treasures of the Study

Four Treasures of the Study refers to the four items used in Chinese calligraphy by men of letters in the study, i.e. the brush, ink, paper and ink stone.

The most widely used writing tool in the Middle Ages in the West

The quill pen, the dominant writing instrument in the Middle Ages, was in use from the 7th century to the 19th century. The quill pen was made of bird feathers, the best of which were from living swans, turkeys and geese.

Discussion

1. Do you think it necessary to write a good hand of Chinese characters nowadays? Why or why not?
2. If you would like to invite some international colleagues to your birthday party, will you write the invitation with a brush, a pen or simply send an electronic one? State your reasons.

玖　王羲之爱鹅

引

王羲之（公元 303 年—公元 361 年），魏晋人，是公认的史上最伟大的书法家。他擅长各种书法，尤善草体。

在浙江省天台山的国清寺里，有一块石碑上刻着一个“鹅”字。这个“鹅”字非常特别，只用一笔连贯写成。然而，这个独笔“鹅”字却只有一半是王羲之真迹，另一半由书法家曹抡补写。他花了七年时间研究、临摹王羲之的书法，最终把“鹅”字的另一半补得浑然天成。

⊙ 独笔“鹅”石碑
位于浙江天台山国清寺

故事

“书圣”王羲之尤其爱鹅。

有一次他得知有位老妇人养了一只十分可爱的鹅，便派人去买，但是这位老人却不肯卖。王羲之有点失望，便决定邀请友人一同去观赏。

听说有贵客要来，老太太受宠若惊，决定盛情款待。王羲之到了老太太家，一眼便看见了盘子里的鹅。他伤心欲绝，说不出话来，终日叹息。

另外一个故事是关于一个道士。道士非常想要本王羲之手抄版《道德经》。王羲之当时已经名扬天下，他知道这并非易事。于是道士就想了一个“计谋”。他养了一群白鹅，并常常到王羲之与友人郊游处放鹅。

终于有一天，大书法家王羲之“偶遇”了那群白鹅。那些鹅步态优雅，立刻就吸引住王羲之的注意。他提出要买，道士却悠悠回答：“我的鹅不卖。不过你如果愿意帮我书写一本《道德经》，我倒可以考虑以鹅相赠。”

王羲之当即挥毫，给道士手抄了一份《道德经》，然后带着他的鹅欢喜而归。

◎ 元朝钱选作《王羲之观鹅图》局部
美国纽约大都会艺术博物馆藏品

文化链接

古代文人雅好

古代文人有许多雅好，既反映出他们的生活情趣，又体现出他们的人生态度。

2006 年，湖北省出土的元朝文物青花瓷器上，分别绘制“王羲之爱兰”，“陶渊明爱菊”，“周敦颐爱莲”，“林和靖爱梅鹤”四图，故名《四爱图》。

◎ 青花瓷瓶上的《四爱图》
湖北武汉湖北博物馆藏品

汉字字体

汉字书法有不同字体，主要包括：篆书、隶书、楷书、行书、草书。欧阳询、颜真卿、柳公权和赵孟頫被称为“楷书四大家”。

◎ 篆书

◎ 隶书

◎ 楷书

◎ 行书

◎ 草书

◎ 欧体

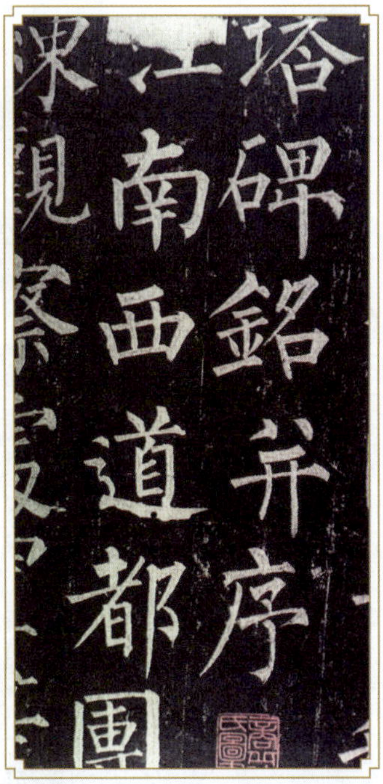

◎ 柳体

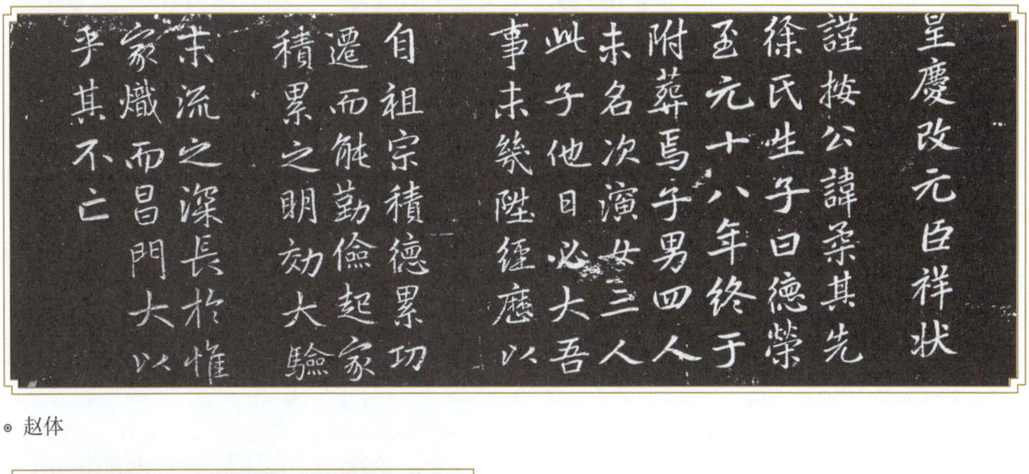

◎ 赵体

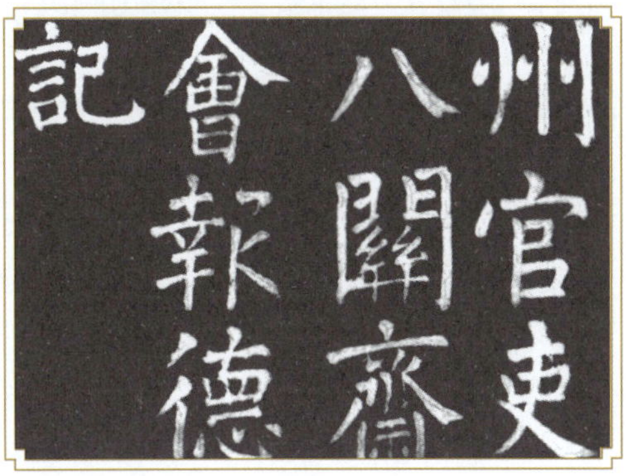

◎ 颜体

文房四宝

文房四宝指文人书房中写书法时需用到的四件物品，即：笔墨纸砚。

中世纪西方的主要书写工具

羽毛笔，中世纪最主要的书写工具，使用时间从公元 7 世纪到公元 19 世纪。羽毛笔由鸟类的羽毛制成，最佳种类有天鹅、火鸡或鹅的羽毛。

讨论

1. 你觉得当今写一手漂亮的书法还有必要吗？为什么？
2. 假如你想邀请一些外国同事参加你的生日聚会，你会选择用毛笔还是钢笔写请柬，或者索性发电子邮件呢？请给出理由。

X XIE DAOYUN COMPARING SNOWFLAKES TO WILLOW CATKINS

Introduction

Xie Daoyun (c. 335AD–c. 405AD), born into the distinguished Xie clan in the Jin Dynasty, is one of the ten female talents in ancient China.

It is recorded she once managed to help her brother-in-law Wang Xianzhi out by forceful argument; during Sun En Rebellion, she took the armor and led her family's fighting against the rebels.

⊙ The picture of Xie Daoyun, painted in the Qing Dynasty

◉ The museum in memory of Wang Dao and Xie An, located at the Wuyi Lane in Nanjing in Jiangsu Province

Story Time

In Wuyi Lane of Stone City (present Nanjing City), there lived one of the most notable families—Xie clan. Xie An, who was the prime minister then, placed great emphasis on family education. He always spent time with the children of his family and quizzed them on literature.

One cold winter day, inky clouds filled the sky, bitterly cold. Xie An gathered juniors of the family to discuss literature as usual.

Then, a tiny bit of snowflakes began to float down. As the conversation went on, the snow became heavier and heavier. A little while later, there was a vast expanse of whiteness out of the window. Looking into the distance, Xie An blurt out willingly, "What does the swirling snow look like?"

His nephew, Xie Lang, with a reputation of having great literary talents, answered immediately, "It is like sprinkling salt into the air." Exactly, the snow was sparkling and crystal-clear, like the salt. Hearing Xie Lang making a proper figure of speech, Xie An nodded his head gently.

His niece Xie Daoyun continued, "More like willow catkins flying high." She compared the heavy snow to the willow catkins fluttering in the sky, profusely and disorderly. How clever it was! Upon hearing this, Xie An laughed in appreciation. At that time, Xie Daoyun was only about seven years old.

This is also the origin of "the woman with a talent for composing verses about catkin." People of later generations always use this idiom to refer to talented women.

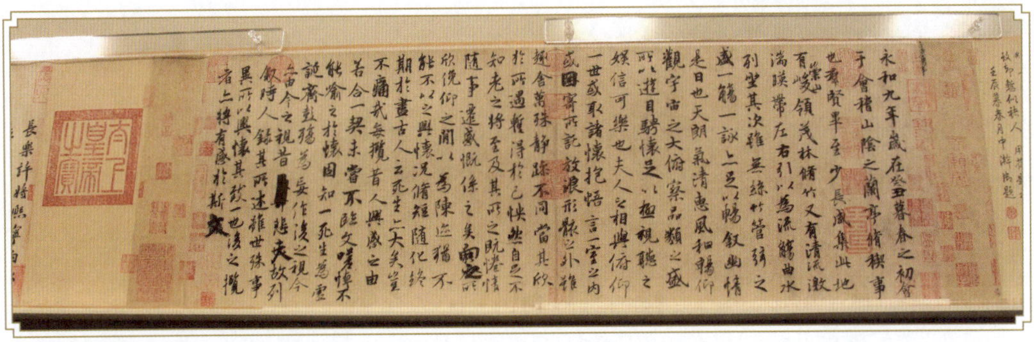

The main text of a Tang Dynasty copy of Wang Xizhi's *Lantingji Xu* by Feng Chengsu, held by the Palace Museum in Beijing

Cultural Links

The literature in the Jin Dynasty

Both Wang Xizhi and Xie Daoyun were literary talents in the Jin Dynasty (266 AD–420 AD). Though frequently in the political instability and social unrest, the Jin Dynasty was a dynamic period in the history of Chinese literature. Generally speaking, the literary talents at that time liked to use flowery speech and the antithetical parallelism, and some of them had a great impact on the later masters, such as Wang Wei, Li Bai, Su Shi, etc.

Some representative works in the Jin Dynasty are listed as follows.

Lu Ji: *Wen Fu*

Zuo Si: *Fu on the Three Capitals*

Gan Bao: *In Search of the Supernatural: The Written Record*

Chen Shou: *Records of the Three Kingdoms*

Wang Xizhi: *A Letter to Xie An; Lantingji Xu*

Guo Pu: *Fu on the Yangtze River; Wandering as an Immortal*

Tao Yuanming: *Peach Blossom Spring*

Folk legend: *Liang Shanbo and Zhu Yingtai*

The Wuyi Lane

Located on the side of the Qinhuai River in Nanjing, the Wuyi Lane is an ancient lane with the longest history in China. During the period of the Three Kingdoms, it was the barracks of the army guarding the Stone City of the Wu State. The name Wuyi means black clothes since non-commissioned officers at that time always dressed in black. The distinguished families of the Jin Dynasty lived here, including Wang Xizhi's and Xie An's. The renowned poem *The Wuyi Lane* composed by Liu Yuxi of the Tang Dynasty was based on it.

Wuyi Lane

A Shakespeare's poem containing the figure of speech

Sonnet 18 by Shakespeare

Shall I compare thee to a summer's day?
Thou art more lovely and more temperate.
Rough winds do shake the darling buds of May,
And summer's lease hath all too short a date.
Sometime too hot the eye of heaven shines,
And often is his gold complexion dimmed;
And every fair from fair sometimes declines,
By chance or nature's changing course untrimmed.
But thy eternal summer shall not fade
Nor lose possession of that fair thou ow'st;
Nor shall Death brag thou wand'r'st in his shade,
When in eternal lines to time thou grow'st.
So long as men can breathe or eyes can see,
So long lives this, and this gives life to thee.

Discussion

1. Besides Xie Daoyun's own talent, what do you think makes her famous?
2. Could you find more figures of speech in the famous literary works? List some.

拾　谢道韫咏絮

引

谢道韫（约公元 335 年—约公元 405 年）出生于晋朝名门谢家，中国古代十大才女之一。

据载，谢道韫曾舌战群儒，帮小叔王献之解围；孙恩叛乱时，她执刀仗剑，带领家人与叛乱者抗衡。

◎ 谢道韫画像
清朝画作

◎ 王导谢安纪念馆
位于江苏南京乌衣巷中

故事

在石头城（现南京）的乌衣巷，居住着当时的大户人家谢氏家族。谢安是当时的宰相，很重视家教家风。他常和小辈们在一起，时不时考考他们的文才。

寒冬的一天，乌云密布，寒风凛冽，谢安如常聚齐家中子女，讲论文义。

这时，外面雪花开始一星半点地下起来。在他们谈天说地时，雪越下越大。不一会儿，窗外就白茫茫的一片了。谢安看着窗外，欣然问道："白雪纷纷何所似？"

素有"文义艳发"美誉的侄子谢郎立即答道："撒盐空中差可拟。"确实，雪花粉白晶莹，如盐一般。听到谢郎比喻恰当，谢安略微点了点头。

侄女谢道韫接着说道："未若柳絮因风起。"她把大雪比作柳絮，纷纷扬扬，多么精妙啊！谢安听后，大笑称赞。当时，谢道韫才七岁。

这也是"咏絮之才"的由来，后来人们用此成语形容有才华的女性。

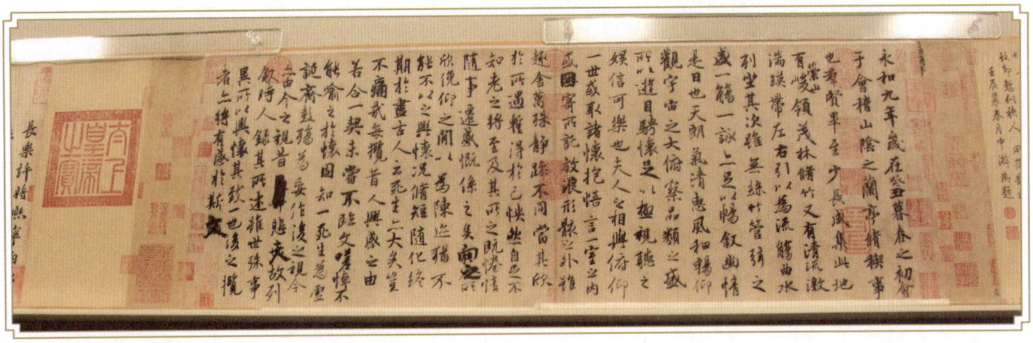

◎ 唐朝冯承素临王羲之《兰亭集序》的主体部分
北京故宫博物馆藏品

文化链接

晋朝文学

王羲之和谢道韫都是晋朝（公元266年—公元420年）文人。尽管时局动荡不稳，但在中国文学史上，晋朝却是非常活跃的阶段。当时的文学才子们一般都喜欢用华丽辞藻和工整对偶，其中有些文人对之后的王维、李白、苏轼等文学名家产生了极大影响。

晋朝的部分文学代表作如下：

陆机:《文赋》

左思:《三都赋》

甘宝:《搜神记》

陈寿:《三国志》

王羲之:《与谢安书》《兰亭集序》

郭璞:《江赋》《游仙诗》

陶渊明:《桃花源记》

民间传说:《梁山伯与祝英台》

乌衣巷

乌衣巷位于南京秦淮河边，是中国历史最悠久的古巷。这里曾是三国时期吴国禁卫军驻地。巷名“乌衣”的意思是黑色的衣服，由于当时军士总穿着黑衣，由此得名。晋朝时，乌衣巷是包括王羲之和谢安家族在内的世家大族居住地。唐朝诗人刘禹锡依此作成名诗《乌衣巷》。

◎ 乌衣巷

包含比喻的莎士比亚诗作

《莎士比亚十四行诗第十八首》

我怎么能够把你来比作夏天?
你不独比它可爱也比它温婉:
狂风把五月宠爱的嫩蕊作践,
夏天出赁的期限又未免太短:
天上的眼睛有时照得太酷烈,
它那炳耀的金颜又常遭掩弊:
被机缘或无常的天道所摧折,
没有方艳不终于凋残或销毁。
但是你的长夏永远不会凋落,
也不会损失你这皎洁的红芳,
或死神夸口你在他影里漂泊,
当你在不朽的诗里与时同长。
只要一天有人类,或人有眼睛,
这诗将长存,并且赐给你生命。

(梁宗岱译)

讨论

1. 除了谢道韫自身的天赋,你认为还有哪些因素成就了她?
2. 在文学名篇中你还能找出更多的比喻吗?请列举一些。

XI ZU CHONGZHI AND *PI*

Introduction

In 1967, a bowl-shaped lunar crater on the far side of the moon was named after Zu Chongzhi (429 AD–500 AD) by the International Astronomical Union, in honor of the prominent Chinese mathematician and astronomer.

On 9 November 1964, a minor planet discovered by the Purple Mountain Observatory in the same year was named after the great scientist as Asteroid Zu Chongzhi, whose international permanent number is 1888.

◎ "Biography of Zu Chongzhi" in the *Book of Southern Qi* written by Xiao Zixian during the Southern Dynasty, held by the National Museum of China in Beijing

Story Time

Zu Chongzhi was a well-known Chinese mathematician and astronomer in the Southern and Northern Dynasties. From early childhood, Zu had shown a strong interest in mathematics.

On one late night when he was five years old, Zu was unable to fall asleep, pondering over what he was taught in the daytime. "Is the circumference of a circle really three times the length of its diameter?" Little Zu Chongzhi could not convince himself of this belief, so he decided to seek the truth.

Next morning, when the day just broke, the boy ran toward the road near the village, with a long rope in hand, waiting for the passing wagons. Finally, he was excited to see a wagon stopping before him. He first measured the circumference of a wheel and then folded the rope into three equal parts. With one part as a benchmark, he measured the diameter of the wheel. After several times' trial, he found the diameter was always a bit shorter than one-third of the circumference.

He made up his mind to work out the mystery. In the following years, he studied Liu Hui's cyclonic method, with which the approximation of *Pi* had been computed to 3.14. Zu admired this method so much that he was determined to continue the work.

After years of efforts, Zu Chongzhi managed to compute *Pi* between 3.1415926 and 3.1415927, which was accurate to seven decimal places. He also gave two other approximations of *Pi*: 355/113 (close ratio) and 22/7 (approximate ratio). *Pi* is also known as *Zu's Ratio* for the great contributions Zu has made to it.

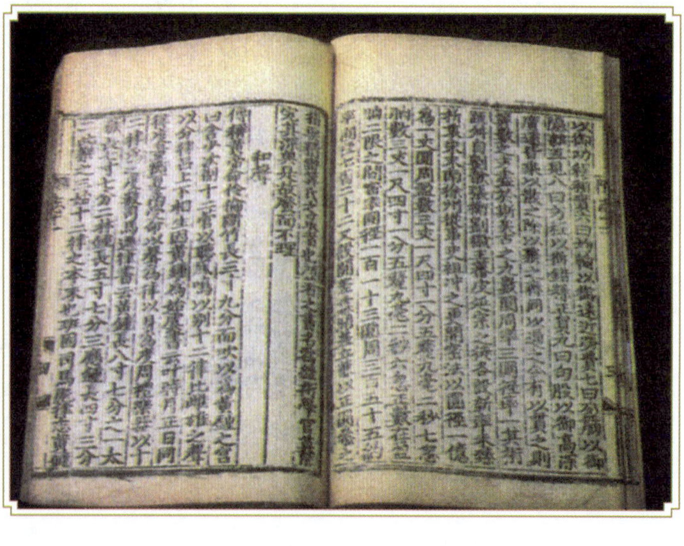

◉ The text about *Zu's Ratio*, written in the "Treatise of Rhythm and the Calendar" in the *Book of Sui*

Cultural Links

Zu Chongzhi's major achievements

Zu Chongzhi's major achievements were in mathematics, astronomy and machinery. He computed the value of *Pi* precise to seven decimal places, calculated a year as 365.24281481 days, and reinvented the south-pointing vehicle, the technology of which had been lost since the Jin Dynasty.

His achievements were closely related to the social background at that time. The Northern and Southern Dynasties (420 AD–589 AD) were divided into the Southern Dynasty, governed by the Han, and the Northern Dynasty, mainly by the Xianbei. Each state developed a series of policies to advance the science and technology, trying to guarantee the dominant position in the political chaos.

Mathematics from ancient Chinese perspective

The ancient Chinese were good at raising and solving mathematics problems. For example, thousands of years ago, a rather complicated problem was raised:

Certain items are purchased jointly. If each person pays eight coins, the surplus is three coins, and if each person gives seven coins, the deficiency is four coins. Find the number of people and the total cost of the items.

(Key: There are seven people and the total cost of the item is 53 coins.)

This problem was recorded in *The Nine Chapters on the Mathematical Art*, one of the oldest and the most influential mathematical texts in China.

Comments on mathematics and mathematicians

The enchanting charms of this sublime science reveal only to those who have the courage to go deeply into it. — Carl Friedrich Gauss

The pure mathematician, like the musician, is a free creator of his world of ordered beauty. — Bertrand Russell

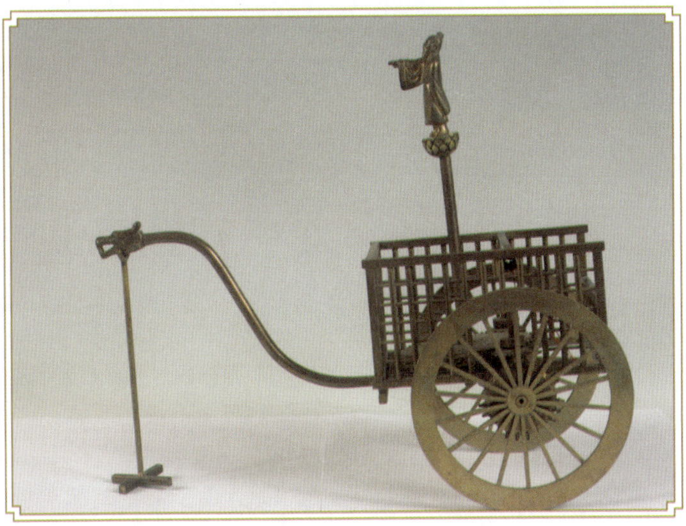

⊙ The model of south-pointing vehicle, exhibited in the National Museum of China in Beijing

Discussion

1. How science and liberal art contribute to the world civilization?
2. What are the essential qualities to be a great mathematician?

拾壹　祖冲之与圆周率

引

1967 年，为了纪念中国杰出的数学家及天文学家祖冲之（公元 429 年—公元 500 年），国际天文学家联合会把月球上的一座环形山命名为“祖冲之环形山”。

1964 年 11 月 9 日，紫金山天文台将 1964 年发现的国际永久编号为 1888 的小行星命名为“祖冲之星”。

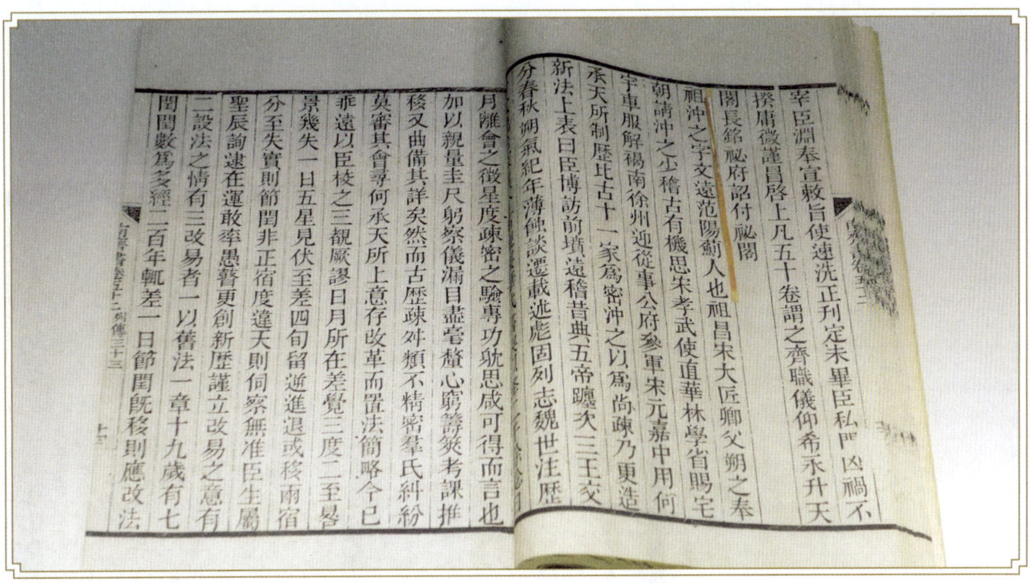
宰臣淵奉宣敕旨使速洗正刊定未畢臣私門凶禍不
撰唐徵謹冒啓上凡五十卷謂之齊職儀仰希永升天
閣長銘祕府詔付祕閣
祖沖之字文遠范陽薊人也祖昌宋大匠卿父朔之奉
朝請沖之少稽古有機思宋孝武使直華林學省賜宅
宇車服解褐南徐州迎從事公府參軍宋元嘉中用何
承天所制歷比古十一家爲密沖之以爲尚疏乃更造
新法上表曰臣博訪前墳遠稽昔典五帝躔次三王交
分春秋朔氣紀年薄蝕談遷載述彪固列志魏世注歷
月離會之徵星度疏密之驗專功覃思咸可得而言也
加以親量圭尺躬察儀漏目盡毫氂心窮籌筴考課推
移又曲備其詳矣然而古歷疏舛頗不精密羣氏糾紛
莫審其會尋何承天所上意存改革而置法簡略今已
乖遠以臣校之三覩厥謬日月所在差覺三度二至晷
景幾失一日五星見伏至差四旬留逆進退或移兩宿
分至失實則節閏非正宿度違天則伺察無准臣生屬
聖辰詢逮在運敢率愚瞽更創新歷謹立改易之意有
二設法之情有三改易者一以舊法一章十九歲有七
閏閏數爲多經二百年輒差一日節閏既移則應改法

◎ 南朝萧子显著《南齐书·祖冲之传》
北京中国国家博物馆藏品

故事

祖冲之是南北朝时期著名的数学家和天文学家，自幼就对数学有浓厚兴趣。

五岁时的一个夜晚，祖冲之躺在床上辗转难眠，回想着白天所学的知识。“圆周长真的等于圆直径的三倍吗？”年幼的祖冲之难以信服，决定去寻求真相。

第二天，天刚破晓，他就手持长绳，迫不及待地跑到大路旁边，等待过往的车辆。终于，一辆马车停在了他面前。他十分兴奋，先用绳子测量了车轮周长，然后把绳子折成三等分，以此为标准来测量车轮直径。几经尝试，他发现车轮的直径总比圆周长的三分之一要短些。

他决心要解开这个谜。后来的几年中，祖冲之研究了刘徽的“割圆术”，刘徽用这个方法将 π 值粗确到了 3.14。祖冲之十分钦佩“割圆术”，决定用此法继续研究下去。

经多年努力，祖冲之成功地将圆周率计算到 3.1415926 和 3.1415927 之间，精确到小数点后面七位。他还给出了另外两个圆周率近似值：355/113（密率）和 22/7（约率）。由于祖冲之对圆周率的巨大贡献，后人又把圆周率成为“祖率”。

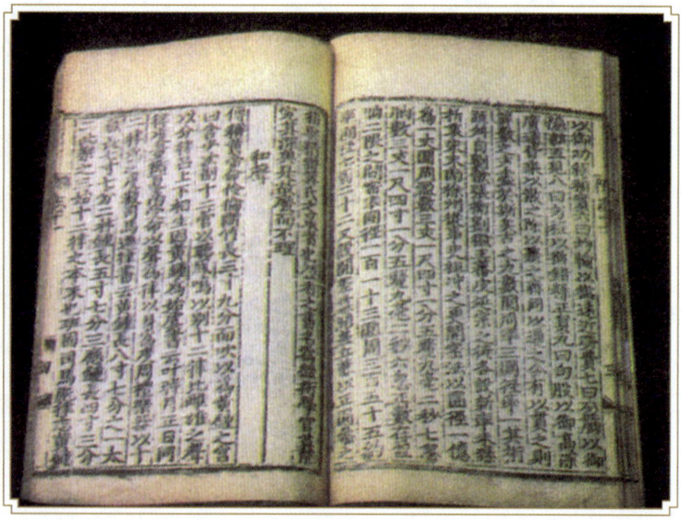

◎ 有关“祖率”的记载
《隋书·律历志》选文

文化链接

祖冲之的主要成就

祖冲之的主要成就在数学、天文学及机械三方面。他计算出的 π 值精确到小数点后面七位；他计算出一年是 365.24281481 天；他重新发明了晋朝后失传的指南车技术。

祖冲之的成就与当时的社会背景是分不开的。南北朝（公元 420 年—公元 589 年）分为汉族政权统治的南朝和主要由鲜卑族统治的北朝。在政治动荡中，各国纷纷推出一系列政策，推进科技发展，以确保自己的统治地位。

古人看数学

古代中国人非常善于提出并解决数学问题，几千年前就曾提出过一个相当复杂的数学问题：

“今有共买物，人出八，盈三；人出七，不足四。问人数物价各几何？”

（答案是：有七人，物价五十三）。

该问题记录于中国最古老也是最有影响力的一本数学专著——《九章算术》。

名家说数学

数学之崇高魅力，唯入其中者方可领略。——卡尔·弗雷德雷克·高斯

纯粹的数学家，正如音乐家一样，自由创造着自己世界的秩序之美。——伯特兰·罗素

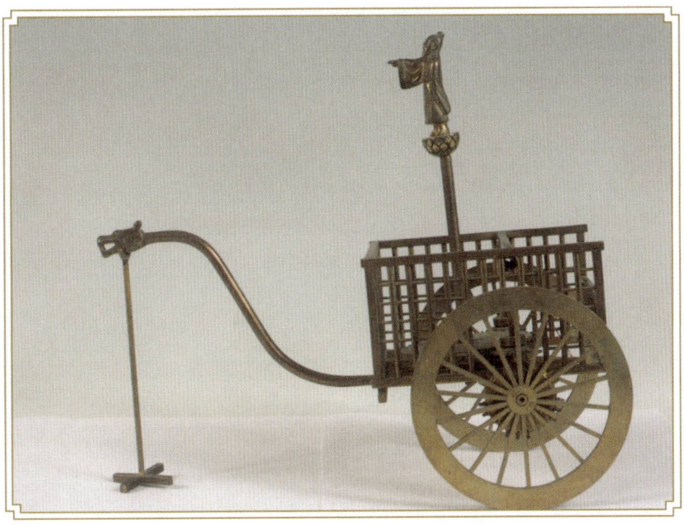

◎ 指南车模型
北京中国国家博物馆展品

讨论

1. 科学和人文是如何影响世界文明进程的?

2. 你认为一名伟大数学家所必需的基本素养有哪些?

XII DANCE OF RAINBOW SKIRT AND FEATHERED GOWN

Introduction

Dance of Rainbow Skirt and Feathered Gown is a traditional dance dating from the Tang Dynasty in ancient China. The music was composed by Emperor Xuanzong of Tang (685 AD–762 AD) and the movements were invented by his love Yang Yuhuan (719 AD–756 AD), also known as Consort Yang. The dance is mentioned in a poem written by the famous Tang Dynasty poet Bai Juyi, "Of all the thousands of court dances, I like most the *Dance of Rainbow Skirt and Feathered Gown*."

⊙ A Tang Dynasty dancing girl's *Dance of Rainbow Skirt and Feathered Gown*, included in the *Images of Unrivaled Beauties for Centuries* painted in the Ming Dynasty

Story Time

On a Mid-Autumn night, the moon was as bright as silver. Emperor Xuanzong enjoyed the glorious full moon in the Daming Palace, unconsciously drifting off to sleep.

All of a sudden, he came into an unfamiliar palace that was partly hidden and partly visible in the cloud and mist. On the top of the gate, there inscribed "Moon Palace."

Emperor Xuanzong was so pleasantly surprised that he could not wait to set foot in. At that moment came a piece of melodious music of flute from indoors. The low-pitched tunes gradually became deep, sometimes clear, and sometimes mild. Then, a variety of other musical instruments joined in. Deeply attracted by the beautiful music, he quickened his pace and saw fairies in rainbow-colored and feathered costumes dancing.

At this point, one court maid waked him up and reminded him to go back to rest in the bedroom. Emperor Xuanzong was brought back to the real world. Next day, he felt that the heavenly music long lingered on, so he tried to recall the melody. Just at that time, Yang Jingshu, the governor of Xiliang, sent *Brahmin Song of Western Regions* as tribute to him. To his surprise, the music style was so similar to that in his dream. Emperor Xuanzong combined both and finally composed the melody, which was given by him the name *Music of Rainbow Skirt and Feathered Gown*.

⊙ The painting depicting Emperor Xuanzong and Consort Yang with attendants on a terrace, painted by Japanese painter Kanō Eitoku

Yang Yuhuan, Xuanzong's beloved consort, was also a talented musician and dancer. At the ceremony when she was conferred the title of Imperial Consort, she danced to the *Music of Rainbow Skirt and Feathered Gown*. This dance is known as the Dance of Rainbow Skirt and Feathered Gown, which incorporates traditional Chinese and Central Asian dance elements. Graceful and enchanting, it is in perfect harmony with the music.

Cultural Links

The Daming Palace of the Tang Dynasty

The Tang Dynasty (618 AD–907 AD) is generally regarded as a high point in China's history, as well as a golden age of cosmopolitan culture. The Tang capital at Chang'an (present Xi'an of Shaanxi Province) was the biggest and most popular city in the world. Thereafter, people overseas often called Chinese "Tang people."

The Daming Palace, the imperial palace of the Tang Dynasty, was the most magnificent palace complex in the world. The Daming Palace covers an area of about three times that of Versailles in France, 13 times that of Kremlin in Russia, and 15 times that of the Buckingham Palace in the U.K. It reaches a peak of Chinese palace architecture, casting great influence on later palace buildings in China and other Asian countries. This historic site was included in the World Heritage List in 2014.

⊙ The historic site of the Daming Palace in Xi'an in Shaanxi Province

Plump Huan and Slender Yan

Both Huan and Yan are ancient Chinese beauties. Huan refers to Yang Yuhuan in the Tang Dynasty, who was said to be plump and so beautiful that she put all flowers to shame. Yan refers to Zhao Feiyan, also known as Empress Xiaocheng in the Han Dynasty, who was allegedly slender in an incredibly attractive way. That is how the Chinese idiom "Plump Huan and Slender Yan" comes, which indicates the different aesthetic judgments in different times.

Now this idiom is also applied to domains of arts, indicating that different artistic styles have their own characteristics. For example, Chinese paintings were more realistic in earlier period, but turned to be more impressionistic after the Northern Song Dynasty.

Ballet

Ballet is a type of court dance that originated during the Italian Renaissance in the 15th century. The most important feature of ballet is to dance on the tips of toes. Now, it has become a widespread dance in the world.

◎ *Cranes*, painted by Emperor Huizong of the Song Dynasty

◎ *The Bird and the Flower*, painted by Zhu Da of the Qing Dynasty

Discussion

1. Why did Chinese people prefer plump beauties in the Tang Dynasty? Try to find some possible reasons.
2. Do you know any other forms of dancing? Try to name some.

拾贰　霓裳羽衣舞

引

《霓裳羽衣舞》是一种中国传统舞蹈。该舞蹈创编于唐朝，由唐玄宗（公元685年—公元762年）编曲，妃子杨玉环（公元719年—公元756年）编舞。杨玉环也被称为“杨贵妃”。唐诗人白居易曾作诗说道：“千歌万舞不可数，就中最爱霓裳舞”。

◎ 跳霓裳羽衣舞的唐朝舞女
明朝《千秋绝艳图》画作局部

故事

一个中秋夜，月如银盘，唐玄宗在大明宫内赏月，不知不觉沉沉睡去。

突然，他来到了一个陌生的宫殿，这里云雾缭绕，若隐若现，门楣上刻着三字“广寒宫”。

玄宗心里高兴，迫不及待想去探个究竟。这时，一阵清脆悦耳的笛声从宫中传来。曲调由低沉渐转高亢，时而清脆，时而轻柔。之后，各种乐器同时响起，配合着笛声。玄宗被这美妙的音乐深深吸引，他加快了脚步，看到仙女们穿着美丽的霓裳羽衣在翩翩起舞。

此时，一名宫女叫醒了玄宗，请他回寝宫休息。玄宗被拉回现实之中。第二天，玄宗依然觉得仙乐还在耳边久久萦绕，因此他试着回忆起这乐曲。就在这时，西凉都督杨敬述献来西域名曲《婆罗门曲》。让玄宗吃惊的是，这曲子竟和他梦中的仙乐如此相近！玄宗融合了两首曲子，最终作成这首由他命名的曲子：《霓裳羽衣曲》。

◎ 画作中携侍从在露台的唐玄宗和杨贵妃
日本画家狩野永德绘

唐玄宗的爱妃杨玉环在音乐和舞蹈方面很有天赋。在她被册封为“贵妃”的典礼上，《霓裳羽衣曲》响起，她依韵起舞，这就是著名的《霓裳羽衣舞》。杨贵妃的舞蹈结合了本土传统和中亚风情，绰约多姿，和音乐达成了完美的和谐。

文化链接

唐朝皇宫大明宫

唐朝（公元 618 年—公元 907 年）被公认为是中国历史上的强盛时代，是文化开放的黄金时期。唐都长安（今陕西西安）是当时世界上最大和最受欢迎的城市。唐朝之后，海外多称中国人为“唐人”。

唐朝皇宫大明宫，是当时全世界最辉煌壮丽的宫殿群。大明宫的占地面积相当于三个凡尔赛宫、十三个俄罗斯克里姆林宫和十五个白金汉宫。它是中国宫殿建筑的巅峰之作，对后世及其他亚洲国家影响深远。2014 年，大明宫遗址被联合国列入《世界遗产名录》。

陕西西安大明宫遗址

环肥燕瘦

“环”与“燕”是中国古代两位美人。“环”指唐代杨玉环，据说她体态丰腴，有闭月羞花之容；“燕”指汉代赵飞燕，即孝成皇后，据说她身姿纤巧，有倾国倾城之貌。成语“环肥燕瘦”因此而得，说明了不同时代人们审美倾向的差异。

现在这个成语也被用到艺术领域，指不同艺术风格各有所长。例如，早期中国绘画尚写实，北宋后则重写意。以下为两例。

《瑞鹤图》
宋徽宗绘

芭蕾舞

芭蕾源于十五世纪意大利文艺复兴时期的宫廷舞，其最重要的一个特征就是表演时要以脚尖点地。现在，芭蕾舞已成为风靡全球的一种舞蹈。

《花鸟图》
清朝朱耷绘

讨论

1. 为何唐朝时中国人偏好丰腴之美？请试着找出一些原因。
2. 你还知道哪些其他形式的舞蹈吗？请试着讲一下。

XIII LU YU DISTINGUISHING WATER

Introduction

Lu Yu (733 AD–804 AD), abandoned as a baby, was adopted and brought up by a Buddhist monk, Chan master Zhi Ji of the Longgai Monastery. From early childhood, Lu Yu had been taught to brew tea by Zhi Ji and was quite talented in it.

He spent more than 25 years in researching and writing *The Classic of Tea*, the first book on tea in the world. The book consists of 10 chapters, dealing with different aspects of tea, from gathering tea leaves to a variety of tools and utensils used in the boiling and drinking of tea.

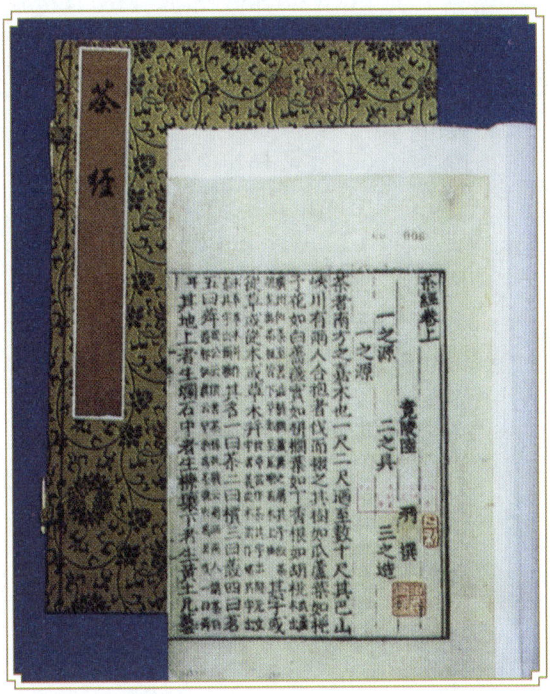

⊙ *The Classic of Tea*, written by Lu Yu

⊙ The portrait of Lu Yu from the *Portraits of Famed Ministers*, compiled during the reign of Emperor Qian Long of the Qing Dynasty

◎ The Zhongling Spring (also Nanling Spring) near the Jinshan Hill in Zhenjiang of Jiangsu, said to have been called Nanling water before the Yangtze River changing its way away from the spring

Story Time

Lu Yu, an outstanding poet and tea master in the Tang Dynasty, was honored as the Sage of Tea. To brew the best tea, he travelled along the middle and lower reaches of the Yangtze River for years, collecting the first-hand material while tasting various kinds of water.

Once, Li Jiqing, the governor of Huzhou, encountered Lu Yu on the Yangtze River, Nanling water in the middle of which was said to be excellent for tea. At that time, Lu Yu's fame of brewing tea had been widely spread. So, the governor would not miss the chance and immediately invited Lu Yu to go aboard his boat.

The governor sent for a minor official to fetch some water from the middle of the river. After a while, a full jar of water was brought before Lu Yu. Ladling the water and pouring it slowly onto the floor, he shook his head and said, "This is not Nanling water. It is more like the water from near the bank." The official knelt on the ground, shocked. "It's my mistake, sir. I had fetched a full jar of water from the middle. But, when I returned, the boat was rocked heavily and only half of the water remained. I knew it was not enough for tea, so I refilled the jar with the water near the bank."

Since then, Lu Yu had become more widely known in China.

⊙ Traditional Chinese tea set

Cultural Links

Classifications of Chinese Tea

Chinese tea, according to the degree of fermentation, roughly falls into four types, which include black tea, green tea, oolong tea and dark tea.

Black tea is fully fermented, the most popular being Qihong and Dianhong, produced in Anhui Province and Yunnan Province respectively.

Green tea is not fermented. Longjing originating in the West Lake area, Hangzhou, Biluochun in Suzhou and Maofeng in Mountain Huangshan are among the best.

Oolong tea usually undergoes partial fermentation. The major producers are in Fujian Province and Taiwan Province. Tieguanyin is a popular oolong tea produced in Anxi, Fujian province.

Dark tea undergoes microbial fermentation for several months or even many years. Pu-erh in Yunnan Province and Anhua dark tea in Hunan Province are among the most famous.

Japan's Sage of Tea — Sen no Rikyu

Tea, originating in China, has developed fully and uniquely in Japan. Japanese teaism has carried its esthetic value for centuries.

Sen no Rikyu, Japan's Sage of Tea, was the greatest contributor to Japanese teaism, who enriched its tea spirit with idea of harmony, respect, purity and tranquility. This tea spirit has since been established and is still popular worldwide today.

◎ Japanese tea utensils

◎ English Tea: a teaport, a cream jug and a full teacup on a saucer

Tea in England

Tea serves as an indispensable part of English culture.

It is recorded that tea was first introduced from China to England in the 16th century. But at that time tea was mainly consumed by the upper class and wealthy merchants. The 18th century saw tea getting its way into ordinary people's lives and from then on, England has become one of the largest tea consumers in the world.

In England, people drink tea in various ways. The most common is to serve it with milk, while some prefer to drink it with lemon or simply drink black tea. Whatever the drinking is, sugar is always a popular addition to it.

◎ English afternoon tea

Discussion

1. Do you think tea bags are enrichment to or a deviation from the traditional Chinese tea culture? State your reasons.
2. Where do you prefer to go with your friends at leisure, a coffee bar or a tea house? State your reasons.

拾叁　陆羽辨水

引

陆羽（公元 733 年—公元 804 年）是一个弃婴，被龙盖寺智积禅师收养并抚养成人。幼时，智积禅师就教他沏茶，陆羽于此也很有天赋。

他花了二十五年多的时间钻研并写成了著作《茶经》，是世界第一部茶学专著。《茶经》共十个章节，阐述了从采茶到煮茶、饮茶器具等关于茶不同方面的内容。

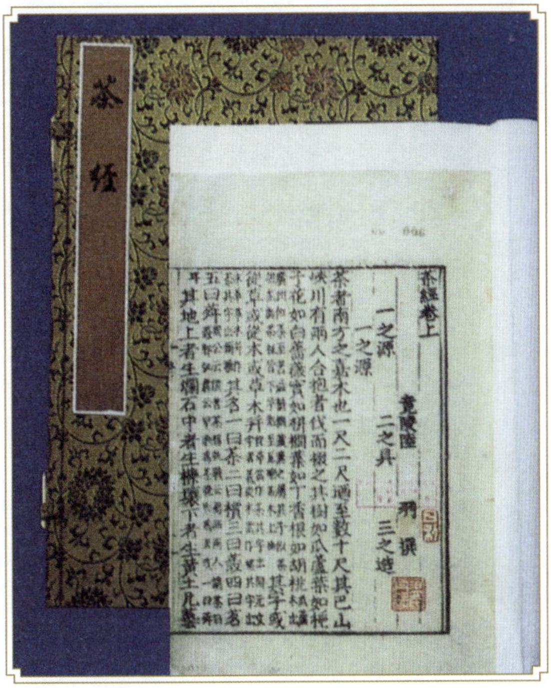

◎《茶经》
陆羽著

◎《历代名臣像解》中的陆羽像
清朝乾隆年间汇编

◎ 江苏镇江金山附近的“中泠泉”（又称“南泠泉”）
据说在长江改道远离泉水之前被称为“南零水”

故事

陆羽，唐朝杰出诗人和烹茶大师，被尊称为“茶圣”。为了沏出好茶，陆羽曾常年行走于长江中下游，搜集一手资料，品鉴各种水源。

一次，湖州刺史李季卿在长江上偶遇陆羽。长江的南零水煮茶据说是天下一绝。当时，陆羽精于茶道已为人所知，刺史不愿错过这个千载难逢的机会，便邀请陆羽同船而行。

刺史当即派小吏去江中心取水。不久，小吏提回了满满的一桶水。陆羽舀了一勺，又慢慢倒在地上，摇头道：“这并非南零水。更像是靠岸边的水啊。”小吏大惊失色，连忙跪在地上说：“我错了，大人。我本在江中取了一罐水，不料回来途中，舟楫摇晃，水洒了一半。我担心这一半的水不够煮茶，便擅自用江边的水将其填满。”

自那以后，陆羽的名字更是被人熟知了。

◎ 中国传统茶具

文化链接

中国茶的分类

中国茶叶根据其发酵程度大致分为四类：红茶、绿茶、乌龙茶和黑茶。

红茶是全发酵茶，最著名的当属安徽祁红和云南滇红。

绿茶属不发酵茶。杭州西湖龙井、苏州碧螺春及黄山毛峰都是绿茶中的翘楚。

乌龙茶经部分发酵，主要产于福建和台湾。安溪铁观音就是产于福建的著名的乌龙茶。

黑茶是经过数月乃至数年的微生物发酵的茶种。黑茶以云南普洱和湖南安化黑茶最为著名。

日本“茶圣”千利休

茶源于中国，传入日本后，日本发展出了自己的特色。几个世纪以来，日本茶道都承载着日本的美学价值。

日本“茶圣”千利休无疑是日本茶道最杰出的贡献者。他倡导的“和敬清寂”丰富了日本的茶道精神。日本的四字茶道精神从此确立，至今仍流行于世。

日本茶道用具

英式茶：茶壶、奶壶和茶碟上倒满茶的茶杯

英格兰茶文化

茶是英格兰文化不可或缺的一部分。

据记载，茶最早于 16 世纪由中国传到英格兰，但当时主要消费人群是上层社会和一些富商。18 世纪开始，茶逐渐进入普通百姓的生活。自那时起，英格兰开始成为世界主要的茶叶消费大国之一。

英格兰人饮茶方式不拘一种。最常见的是在茶里加奶，但也有人爱加柠檬或只喝纯红茶，但无论怎么喝，英格兰人都喜欢在茶里加点糖。

英式下午茶

讨论

1. 你认为袋泡茶是对传统茶道精神的发展还是背离？请陈述理由。
2. 闲暇时你和朋友更愿意去咖啡馆还是茶室？请陈述理由。

XIV SIMA GUANG BREAKING THE VAT

Introduction

Sima Guang (1019–1086), a politician and historian of the Northern Song Dynasty, was diligent and brilliant when he was a boy. The story that 7-year-old Sima Guang broke the vat to save his friend was widely known and commonly seen in paintings on chinaware, jadeware and so on.

◎ The picture of Sima Guang in the *Bibliography of Painting Created in the Wanxiao Hall*, painted by Shangguan Zhou of the Qing Dynasty

⊙ *Sima Guang Breaking the Vat*, standing at the Sima Guang's Former Residence in Xinyang in Henan Province

Story Time

When Sima Guang was a young child, his favorite book was *Zuozhuan*, the commentary on *Spring and Autumn Annals*, written by Zuo Qiuming. By the age of seven, he had been able to retell all the stories in this book and clearly describe the history of over two hundred years clearly. Compared with his peers, Sima Guang showed superior intelligence and more rational calmness.

One day, Sima Guang played hide-and-seek with other children in a garden. A little boy among them saw a large vat at a corner. The boy thought it was so large and deep that nobody could find him. Without hesitation, he dashed out and climbed up the vat stepping on a big stone beside.

Unexpectedly, the large vat was full of water. As its upper edge was narrow, as well as slippery, the little boy fell inside. Soaked in the deep water, he struggled to cry for help. Shocked by the scene and not knowing what to do, other children felt scared and scattered. Some cried, some shouted and some ran outside of the garden, trying to seek help from adults.

The sound in the vat gradually grew fainter and fainter. Just then, a good idea occurred to Sima Guang who still remained there. He lifted the big stone beside and slammed it into the vat. The water leaked out and the boy was finally saved from drowning.

The story about Sima Guang's bravery, calmness and tact quickly spread over the cities of Bianjing and Luoyang, which was portrayed in many paintings at that time.

Later, Sima Guang became a successful scholar and officer, who has been best known for his masterwork *Comprehensive Mirror in Aid of Governance*.

Cultural Links

The first professional fire brigade in the world

People in ancient China often filled the vat with water for fire protection.

In China's history, the Song Dynasty (960 AD–1279) was an era when the economy, culture, education, technology and science were highly prosperous. As the capital city, Bianjing (present Kaifeng city in Henan Province) was crowded with people, houses and shops. Thus, fires broke out frequently, which arouse public concern. Thus, the Song government decided to improve its public service by forming a fire brigade, which was the first professional fire brigade in the world.

Comprehensive Mirror in Aid of Governance

It is a historical work finished by Sima Guang. The book covers the history of about 1,400 years from the Warring States Period to the Five Dynasties. Different from the biographical style of *Records of the Grand Historian*, it is China's first annalistic comprehensive history book. It also casts a great influence on later Chinese historical writings.

A story about a quick-witted boy in Belgium

In downtown Brussels, the capital of Belgium, there stands the Manneken Pis statue depicting a urinating boy named Julianske. Back in the 15th century, the invaders lit the fuse, attempting to blow up Brussels. The boy showed resourcefulness in the emergency—he peed on the burning fuse, quenched it and thus saved the whole city.

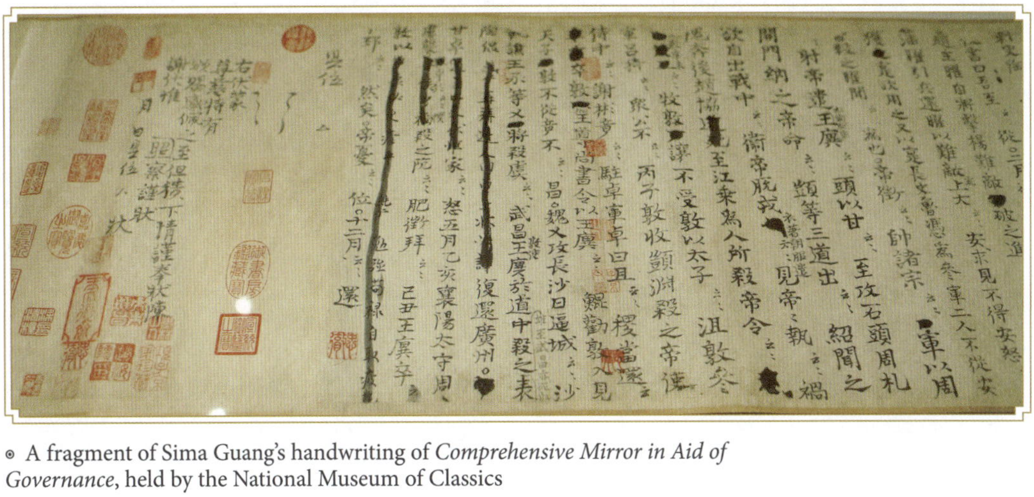

A fragment of Sima Guang's handwriting of *Comprehensive Mirror in Aid of Governance*, held by the National Museum of Classics

Discussion

1. What do you learn from the story of Sima Guang Breaking the Vat?
2. Can you come up with new ideas to save the little boy in the vat in Sima Guang's story? Try to give a description.

拾肆　司马光砸缸

引

司马光（1019 年—1086 年），北宋政治家、史学家。从小勤勉惜时，智力超群。七岁司马光砸缸救友的故事在中国家喻户晓，也是瓷器、玉器装饰画上常见的题材。

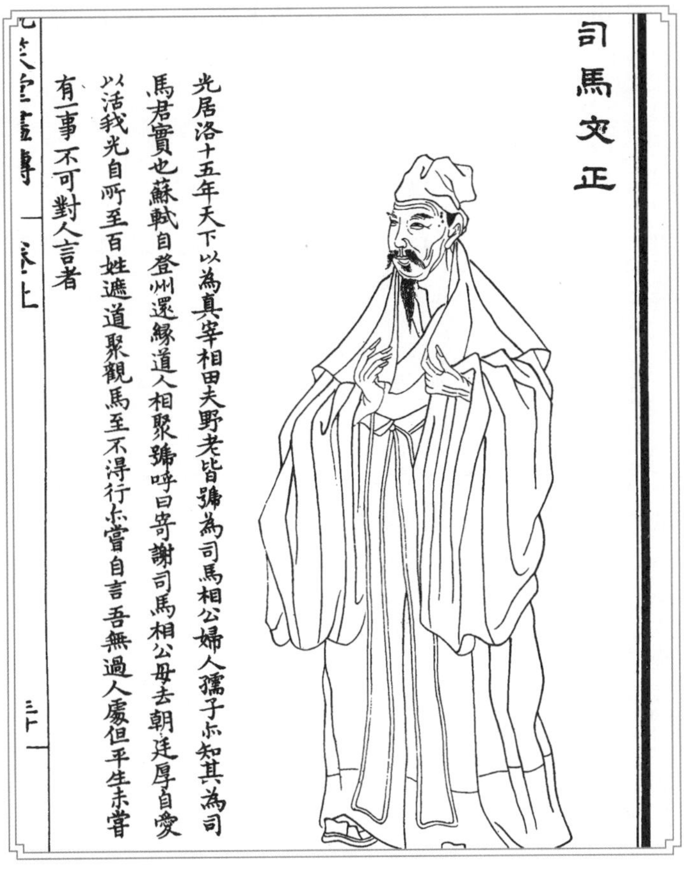

◎《晚笑堂画传》中的司马光画像
清朝上官周绘

◎《司马光砸缸》
河南信阳司马光故居内

故事

司马光小时候非常喜欢读《左传》。七岁时，他便能熟练背诵这本书，并能把两百多年的历史讲得清清楚楚。相比同龄人，司马光聪颖过人，成熟冷静。

一次，司马光和别的小朋友一起在院子里玩捉迷藏。其中一个小男孩想躲到角落的大缸里，觉得那缸又大又深，谁都找不到他。他毫不犹豫地跑过去踩着旁边的一块大石头爬了上去。

谁知，那大缸里装满了水，而缸边又窄又滑，小男孩竟跌入缸中。缸水很深，小男孩只得挣扎呼救。其他孩子见此情景都吓坏了，一哄而散：有的哭，有的喊，还有的跑到外面想找大人帮忙。

缸中的声音越来越弱。留在原地的司马光急中生智，抱起旁边的那块大石头，使劲朝水缸砸去。缸中的水倾泻而出，男孩获救了。

有关司马光勇敢冷静、急中生智的故事在汴京和洛阳城很快传开了，当时很多画者还将此事绘制入画。

后来，司马光很早就成了有名的文人，也做了官，而最为知名的是他的巨著《资治通鉴》。

文化链接

世界第一支专业消防队

在中国古代，人们常用缸蓄水防火。

宋朝（公元 960 年—1279 年）是中国历史上经济、文化、教育和科技高度繁荣的时期。在宋都汴京（现河南省开封市），人口、民居、商铺密集，火灾时有发生。这已经成为百姓的心头大患。因此，宋朝政府决定成立一支消防队以提升其公共职能。这支消防队也是世界上第一支专业的消防队。

《资治通鉴》

《资治通鉴》是由司马光所著的历史巨著，记载了从战国到五代时期约 1400 年的历史。

不同于纪传体的《史记》，《资治通鉴》是中国第一部编年体通史。它对后世史书写作产生了巨大影响。

比利时男孩急中生智的故事

在比利时首都布鲁塞尔市中心，矗立着撒尿童子小于连的雕像。在十五世纪，当外国入侵者点燃了炸药引线，准备炸毁布鲁塞尔时，小于连在关键时刻急中生智——撒尿浇灭了炸弹引线，拯救了全城。

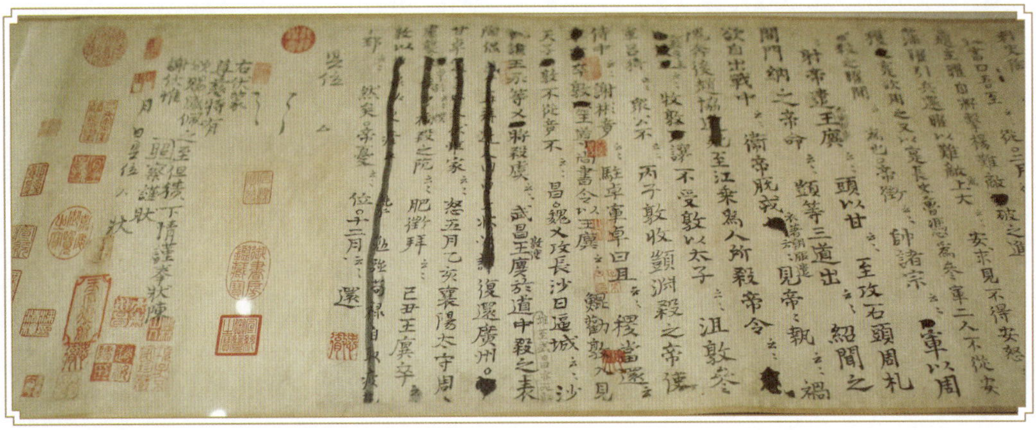

司马光手书《资治通鉴》残稿
国家典籍博物馆藏品

讨论

1. 从《司马光砸缸》的故事中，你学到了什么?
2. 你能想出其他办法救司马光砸缸故事中落入缸中的小男孩吗? 请介绍一下你的办法。

XV SU SHI TAKING THE IMPERIAL EXAMINATION

Introduction

Sansu, or the Three Sus, refers to three well-known poets born into one family in the Song Dynasty, the father Su Xun, the elder brother Su Shi, and the younger brother Su Zhe.

They were first mentioned together by Wang Pizhi in the Song Dynasty. Xun was referred as Senior Su, Shi as Elder Su and Zhe as Younger Su. All of them were among the Eight Literary Masters in the Tang and Song.

A Prime Minister in the Qing Dynasty, Zhang Penghe, wrote a couplet for Sansu Temple in Meishan city, Sichuan Province, which says, "Born into one family were three poets; immortal for the writings are four masters ."

◉ A couplet in the Sansu Temple, situated in Meishan in Sichuan Province

◉ *The Picture of Su Shi, painted* by Sun Kehong of the Ming Dynasty

Story Time

In 1056, nineteen-year-old Su Shi (1037–1101) set out on his journey to Bianjing (present Kaifeng, Henan Province), the capital city of the Northern Song Dynasty, taking an important examination in his life—the Imperial Examination.

The chief examiner then was Ouyang Xiu, a leading figure in the world of letters. During the evaluation, all the names on the test paper were sealed. So, when spotting an excellent discourse on politics, he had no idea who wrote it.

Ouyang studied the essay and thought that it must have been Zeng Gong, for no one else could have ever written in such a natural and unrestrained style in his mind.

Ouyang was just about to rank the essay as number one before he realized that Zeng Gong was his student. He hesitated and found himself in a dilemma. To rate the essay as number one might lead to a rumor that the result was obtained by taking advantage of the mentorship. But not to rate the essay as the best would apparently be unjust.

An imperial examination for Confucian scholars, supervised by Emperor Ming Huang of the Tang Dynasty from a pavilion

Finally, Ouyang Xiu rated it as number two, feeling deeply apologetic. It was not until the roll was released that Ouyang Xiu knew the writer turned out to be Su Shi, a young man he had never heard of. Ouyang Xiu told Su Shi about it regretfully, but to his great surprise, the young man laughed it off without making any complaints.

Deeply impressed by the young man's talent and his broad-mindedness as well, Ouyang Xiu talked to himself, "Such a young talent deserves to excel the others on the scroll." Hence comes the Chinese idiom "to excel others."

Cultural Links

The Imperial Examination

The Imperial Examination was a civil service examination system to select potential officials in ancient China.

The system started in the Sui Dynasty and reached its maturity in the Tang Dynasty. In the Song Dynasty, a three-level system was established, from local to national to court examination. By the Ming Dynasty, it reached the peak and the highest degree of *jinshi* became a necessity for prospective officials. It declined in the Qing Dynasty and was abolished in 1905.

Watching the Results on the Scroll, painted on silk by Qiu Ying of the Ming Dynasty

When the results were released, the candidates in the court examination would gather before the Imperial Examination Center to wait for their names to be ranked on a scroll known as the *jinbang*.

Zhuangyuan, followed by *bangyan* and *tanhua*, is still widely used today, referring to the person ranking the first in an exam. The title has its origin in the imperial examination.

The Eight Great Masters of the Tang and Song Dynasties

The Eight Great Masters of the Tang and Song Dynasties refers to the eight great prose writers: Han Yu and Liu Zongyuan in the Tang Dynasty, Ouyang Xiu, Suxun, Sushi, Suzhe, Wang Anshi and Zeng Gong in the Song Dynasty.

Han Yu and Liu Zongyuan, the advocates of the "Classical Prose Movement", wrote essays in a more direct, colloquial style, which were against a tightly restricted prose form called *pianwen*. The movement was echoed by some prose writers in the Song Dynasty, producing a profound and far-reaching influence on the later literature.

Su Shi's poems

Su Shi was excellent in both *shi* and *ci* forms of poetry, leaving thousands of poems to the world. Most of his poems are in the *shi* style, but his poetic fame was mainly achieved through his *ci* style poems. He was the founder of and one of the most influential figures in the Haofang School and many of his quotes are widely known among the Chinese. *To the Tune of Shuidiaogetou* is an example.

…

But rare is perfect happiness—

The moon does wax, the moon does wane,

And so men meet and say goodbye.

I only pray our life be long,

And our souls together heavenward fly!

(Translated by Lin Yutang)

The impact of China's Imperial Examination on Europe

Patronage was practiced in the Middle Ages of Europe, under which the civil servants did not have to take any examinations to get their official posts. With the discovery of the new marine route, China's systems were soon brought to Europe.

Cruz, a missionary travelling to China in the 16th century, had a strong interest in the Chinese rule that an outstanding scholar naturally makes an official. Then, he introduced China's Imperial Examination system to Europe. People thought that it was due to this system that China had been so well governed.

In 1791, France became the first to follow China's example. Germany adopted a similar method of examination in 1800. In 1853, Britain established the civil service examination system, which has been in use to this day.

Discussion

1. If you were Su Shi, what would you say to Ouyang Xiu?
2. Besides examinations, what other methods of selecting the talented can you think of? List a few.

拾伍　苏轼科考

引

“三苏”指宋朝著名的苏氏三父子，父亲苏洵、兄长苏轼和弟弟苏辙，三位都是诗人。

“三苏”并称最初由宋朝王辟之提及，他将苏洵称为“老苏”，苏轼称为“大苏”，苏辙称为“小苏”。“三苏”均属“唐宋八大家”。

清朝宰相张鹏翮为四川省眉山市三苏祠撰写门联：“一门父子三词客，千古文章四大家”。

◎ 三苏祠门联
位于四川眉山

◎《东坡小像》
明朝孙克宏绘

故事

1056年，19岁的苏轼(1037年—1101年）前往南宋都城汴京（现河南省开封市）参加人生的一次大考——科举考试。

主考官欧阳修是当时的文坛领袖。阅卷时，所有考生的姓名是密封的。因此，当欧阳修批阅到一篇非常欣赏的策论时，他并不知道作者是何人。

他赏读之后心想：一定是曾巩所作！再也不会有第二个人能有如此自然不羁的文风了。

欧阳修正想把这篇文章评为第一，却突然意识到曾巩是自己的学生。他犹豫不决，左右为难。如果评为第一，有人会说利用了师生关系之便。但是，如果不评为第一却显然有失公允。

最终，欧阳修心怀歉意，把此文评为第二。直到放榜时，欧阳修才得知作者竟是一个闻所未闻的年轻人，名叫苏轼。欧阳修遗憾地将此事告知苏轼，但让他吃惊的是，苏轼并无任何怨言，一笑置之。

苏轼的才华和胸襟都让欧阳修赞叹，他感慨道："这样的青年才俊，真该让他出榜于人头地啊。"成语"出人头地"便来源于此。

◎ 儒生参加科举考试
唐明皇坐于亭内监考

文化链接

科举考试

科举制是中国古代用来选拔官员的一种考试制度。

这种制度始于隋，完善于唐。宋朝确立了三级科举制度，即乡试、会试、殿试三级。明朝科举制达到鼎盛，考取最高级别的进士成为入朝做官的必经之路。清朝科举制逐渐衰落，于 1905 年废止。

发榜时，参加殿试的考生聚集在贡院门外，等待“金榜题名”。

状元，指在考试中获得第一名的人，至今仍广为使用，后面分别是榜眼和探花。这个称号即源于科举考试。

《观榜图》
明朝仇英绢画

唐宋八大家

唐宋八大家指的是唐代和宋代八位散文大家：唐代的韩愈、柳宗，宋代的欧阳修、苏洵、苏轼、苏辙、王安石以及曾巩。

韩愈和柳宗元是“古文运动”的倡导者，他们提倡用一种更直接、更口语化的文体，反对形式僵化的骈文。该运动在宋代得到部分散文家的呼应，对后世文学产生了深远的影响。

苏轼诗词

苏轼诗词俱佳，给世人留下几千首诗词。虽然这几千首里大部分是诗，然而他却更以词闻名于世。苏轼是豪放派的创始人，也是最有影响力的豪放派词人之一，他的很多词中国人都耳熟能详。如《水调歌头》：

……

人有悲欢离合，
月有阴晴圆缺，
此事古难全。
但愿人长久，
千里共婵娟。

中国科举制对欧洲的影响

中世纪的欧洲实行赐官制度，官员不用参加任何考试即可被录用。新航路开辟后，中国的制度体系开始传到欧洲。

16 世纪来华的传教士克鲁兹对中国“学而优则仕”的原则产生了浓厚兴趣，他把科举制介绍到欧洲。人们认为正是由于这种制度，中国才治理得如此之好。

1791 年，法国率先效仿中国的人才选拔制度;1800 年，德国采纳了类似的考试制度;1853 年，英国确立公务人员考试制度，沿用至今。

讨论

1. 如果你是苏轼，你会对欧阳修说些什么呢?
2. 除了考试，你能想到其他选拔人才的方式吗? 请举一些例子。

XVI TEMUJIN'S HORSE-RACING STRATEGY

Introduction

The Secret History of the Mongols, listed as the world cultural heritage by the United Nations, is the oldest surviving literary work in the Mongolian language. It was written sometime after the death of Temujin (also known as Genghis Khan) (1162–1227) and was compiled in the Ming Dynasty under the title of *The Secret History of the Yuan Dynasty*. The 12-chapter work gives a detailed account of Temujin's life as well as how the Mongol Empire was created.

⊙ The picture of Temujin, painted on the wall of Genghis Khan Temple in Ulan Hot in Inner Mongolia

⊙ *Mongolian Cavalry and Infantry*, painted by the Persian in the 14th century

Story Time

In 1174, the tribe under the rule of Yesugei, Temujin's father, won a battle. To celebrate the victory, Yesugei hosted a horse-racing event, which was unusual in that the winner would be the last one to reach the terminal.

The horse-riders made every effort to proceed slowly. One hour passed, and then another, but even the fastest riders had hardly covered a few miles. The twilight was falling, and the crowds could not stand still.

Yesugei felt regretful for setting such a rule yet he had to keep his word. Thinking for a while, Yesugei ordered that anyone who could end the race soon should get a high reward, without changing the condition of the slowest horse being the winner.

The crowds racked their brains but were unable to offer any solutions. At this moment, Temujin, a 12-year-old boy, walked to the slow-going horses. He whispered something to each rider and made some special arrangements at the same time. With a loud "Go", the horses flied toward the destination like the released arrows. Within a few minutes, the race was put to an end, and the prize still went to the slowest horse.

Yesugei was very surprised and asked his son how he could manage it. Temujin replied, "My father, there's nothing tricky. I just asked the competitors to ride their rivals' horses and still the slowest horse would get the prize."

With great wisdom and bravery, the boy later grew into a hero of an age, who, in 1206, established the Mongol Empire.

Cultural Links

Khan

Khan, originally meaning "heaven" or "jinni", was widely used to refer to the chiefs by people speaking Altaic languages in ancient North China. The title got its unprecedented fame when Temujin established the Mongol Empire, which he ruled as Genghis Khan.

Tian Ji's Horse-Racing Strategy

Another famous horse-racing story in China's history was about Tian Ji.

Once, the king of Qi State invited Tian Ji to participate in a horse-racing event. Adopting a strategy put forward by his retainer Sun Bin, Tian Ji used his inferior horse to race against the king's best one, his average horse to race with the king's inferior one, and his best horse to race with the king's average one. Thus, he won two out of the three races.

◉ *The Building of the Trojan Horse*, painted by the Italian painter Giulio Romano

The Trojan Horse

The Trojan Horse is a famous tale in ancient Greece. The Greek force sieged the city of Troy for ten years but could not break into it, so they pretended to retreat, leaving a huge wooden horse. Not knowing it was a trick, the Trojans pulled the horse into the city as a victory trophy. That night, the Greeks hidden in the horse crept out and opened the gate. The Greeks entered and destroyed the city of Troy.

Today, a Trojan Horse refers to any trick that causes a target to invite an enemy into a well-protected place.

Discussion

1. Which story do you prefer, Tiemujin's or Tian Ji's horse-racing strategy? State your reasons.
2. "Think different" is an advertising slogan for Apple Incorporation. What do you think is the importance of "think different"?

拾陆　铁木真赛马

引

《蒙古秘史》是现存最古老的蒙古语文献，现已被联合国列为世界文化遗产。该著作创作于铁木真（又称“成吉思汗”）（1162 年—1227 年）逝世之后，在明朝被编纂为《元朝秘史》。这部巨著含有 12 个章节，详尽叙述了铁木真的一生和蒙古帝国创建的过程。

◎ 铁木真画像
位于内蒙古乌兰浩特成吉思汗庙内壁画

◎《蒙古骑兵和步兵》
14世纪波斯人绘制

故事

1174 年，铁木真的父亲也速该率领的部落赢得了一场战役。为了庆祝胜利，也速该举行了一次赛马活动。这次比赛的特别之处在于，最后到达终点的马才能获胜。

选手们都竭尽全力减慢速度。一小时，两小时……时间在流逝，但是最快的骑士也才走了一点点的距离。暮色降临，观众按捺不住了。

也速该后悔制定这条赛规，但又不能食言。他稍作考虑后下令道：谁能尽快结束比赛将获重赏，但不能改变慢者获胜的赛规。

众人绞尽脑汁也没能想出什么方法。这时，十二岁的铁木真走到了逗留不前的马匹前，对每个骑士耳语几句，同时做了一些特别的安排。随着一声令下，骑士们如箭离弦，飞快地向终点奔去。不到几分钟，比赛就结束了，仍是最慢马匹获奖。

也速该非常吃惊，就问儿子是如何做到的。铁木真回答：“父亲，这并不难。我只是让骑士们都骑上他人的马，最慢到达终点的那匹马获胜。”

这个有勇有谋的男孩后来成为了一代枭雄，并于 1206 年建立了蒙古帝国。

文化链接

可汗

可汗，原意指“上天”或“神灵”。中国古代北方阿尔泰语系人民广泛用“可汗”来称呼他们的首领。该称谓在铁木真建立蒙古帝国时广为人知。铁木真在统治时期被称为“成吉思汗”。

◎ 成吉思汗像
14世纪绢画

田忌赛马

另外一个著名的赛马故事是田忌赛马。

一次，齐王邀请田忌参加赛马。田忌采纳了门客孙膑的策略，用自己的劣等马对抗齐王的优等马，用自己的中等马对抗齐王的劣等马，用自己的优等马对抗齐王的中等马。这样，田忌以三局两胜赢得比赛。

《特洛伊木马的建造》
意大利画家朱里诺·罗马诺绘

特洛伊木马

特洛伊木马是古希腊著名传说。希腊军队围困特洛伊长达十年而无法攻下该城。于是他们假装撤退，留下一具巨大的木马。特洛伊守军不知是计，把木马运进城里作为战利品。当天夜里，藏在木马腹中的希腊人悄悄爬出，打开城门。希腊军队攻入，一举摧毁特洛伊城。

现在，“特洛伊木马”指任何可能引来敌人的目标物。

讨论

1. 铁木真赛马和田忌赛马的故事，你更喜欢哪一个？请陈述理由。
2. “非同凡想”（求异思维，逆向思维）是苹果公司的一句广告语，你觉得求异思维的重要性体现在哪里？

XVII MARCO POLO TRAVELING TO CHINA

Introduction

Marco Polo (1254–1324) was an Italian merchant, explorer, and one of the first Europeans to travel the Silk Road to China. In 1275, Marco Polo, together with his father and uncle, arrived in Shangdu (in present Inner Mongolia), the capital of the Yuan Dynasty, and the Polos were received with hospitality by Kublai Khan, the emperor of the Yuan Dynasty.

Marco Polo stayed in China for 17 years, traveling to many places in the southeast and southwest of China. In 1295, they returned to Venice.

⊙ The statue commemorating Marco Polo's visit to Hangzhou, standing in Jiangnan Water Towns Culture Museum in Hangzhou in Zhejiang Province

Story Time

In 1271, Marco Polo, at the age of 17, together with his father and uncle, embarked on their voyage from Venice to China. The Polos wanted to sail straight into China, but the ships there were not seaworthy, so they continued overland through the Silk Road.

After four years' journey with severe hardship, the Polos finally arrived in Shangdu and were welcomed by Kublai Khan into his palace. On reaching the Yuan court, the Polos presented the papal letters and gifts to Kublai Khan, who was pleased with their visit.

Marco, too, impressed Khan, who thought highly of the young man and granted important positions in the emperor's court. Marco's immersion into the Chinese culture enabled him to quickly have a good command of Mongolian and Mandarin.

During his stay in China, Marco visited most provinces of southern and eastern China. He had not only great knowledge about the Mongol empire but incredible wonder. He marveled at the empire's use of paper money, an idea that had failed to reach Europe, and was in awe of its economy and scale of production.

After 17 years in Khan's court, the Polos thought it was time to return to Venice. In 1291, Kublai entrusted Marco with his last duty to escort a Mongol princess to Persia, where she was to marry a Persian prince. In 1293, the Polos arrived at Hormuz and left the Mongol princess with the Persian prince. Then they moved to Trabzon and from that city sailed to Venice. In 1295, after 24 years away from home, the Polos finally returned to Venice, with riches and treasures.

The illustration in the French version of *The Travels of Marco Polo*, published in 1375, depicting Kublai Khan meeting the Polos

Cultural Links

Kublai establishing the Yuan Dynasty

After the Mongols having controlled territories including today's North China for decades, Kublai Khan, grandson of Genghis Khan, founded the Yuan Dynasty in 1271. The Yuan Dynasty (1271–1368) was the first dynasty established by ethnic minorities in China.

The Silk Road

The Silk Road has been a network of trade routes connecting the East and the West for over 2,000 years. The name was derived from the profitable trade in silk conducted along these routes. The concept of the Silk Road refers to the Terrestrial Silk Road, the Maritime Silk Road, and the New Silk Road.

The Terrestrial Silk Road was opened up by the Chinese imperial envoy Zhang Qian through his explorations of Central and Western Asia around 114 BC.

The Maritime Silk Road refers to the maritime section of the historic Silk Road that connects China to the countries along the Indian Ocean, later extending to Egypt and finally to Europe, which began in the 2nd century BC.

The New Silk Road, also known as the Belt and Road, is an initiative to promote trade between China and other countries in Asia, Africa and Europe, which was proposed by China's president Xi Jinping in 2013.

The Travels of Marco Polo

The Travels of Marco Polo is a travelogue written down by Rustichello da Pisa from stories told by Marco Polo, describing Polo's travels through Asia between 1271 and 1295, and particularly his experiences at the court of Kublai Khan.

The book had a significant influence on a series of later Western explorers, including Christopher Columbus, and Vasco da Gama, inspiring them to reach Asia by sea.

Discussion

1. Why did Marco Polo travel a long distance to China?
2. How did Marco Polo's travel to China foster the cultural exchanges between the East and the West?

拾柒　马可波罗在中国

引

马可·波罗（1254 年—1324 年）是意大利著名旅行家和商人，也是最早沿丝绸之路来到中国的欧洲人之一。1275 年马可·波罗与父亲和叔叔到达元朝的都城上都（今内蒙古自治区内），并受到元朝皇帝忽必烈大汗的热情款待。

马可·波罗在中国游历 17 年，访问过当时中国东南和西南地区的许多城市。1295 年，马可·波罗与父亲和叔叔回到威尼斯。

◎ 纪念马可波罗到访杭州的雕像
浙江杭州江南水乡文化博物馆

故事

1271年，马可·波罗随父亲和叔叔从威尼斯启程，踏上了前往中国的旅途。那年他只有17岁。他们最初想直接坐船去中国，但他们的船只却不适于航海。马可·波罗等人无奈只能沿着丝绸之路走陆路去东方。

他们一路艰辛，克服重重困难，终于在4年后到达了元朝上都。元朝皇帝忽必烈大汗邀请他们进入皇宫并接见了他们。马可·波罗等人向忽必烈呈上了罗马教皇的信函和礼物，忽必烈也对他们的来访表示热烈的欢迎。

忽必烈对马可·波罗颇为赞赏，认为他年轻有为，还在朝中赐予他重要的官职。马可·波罗很快融入了中国文化，不久便基本掌握了蒙古语和汉语。

在中国期间，马可·波罗的足迹遍布中国南部和东部大部分城市。尽管他对蒙古帝国所知甚多，但依然充满了好奇之心。当看到在欧洲闻所未闻的纸币时，他大为惊叹。同时，他对元朝的经济情况和生产规模啧啧称奇。

在中国游历了17年后，马可·波罗等人觉得是时候离开中国回到故乡了。1291年，忽必烈下旨让马可·波罗等人护送蒙古公主远嫁波斯，并允许他们完成任务后回国。1293年，他们护送公主到达霍尔木兹，将公主交给波斯王子，随即取道特拉布宗坐船回威尼斯。1295年，在阔别故乡24年后，马可·波罗等人带着大量的金银财宝回到了威尼斯。

1375年法语版《马可波罗游记》插图
描述忽必烈接见马可·波罗等人的情景

文化链接

忽必烈建立元朝

在占领中国北部长达数十年后，蒙古帝国成吉思汗之孙忽必烈于 1271 年建立元朝。元朝（1271 年—1368 年）是中国历史上第一个由少数民族建立的王朝。

丝绸之路

丝绸之路是两千多年来连接东西方的贸易路线。由于该路线最初用于丝绸交易，丝绸之路也由此得名。丝绸之路的概念包括陆上丝绸之路、海上丝绸之路与新丝绸之路。

陆上丝绸之路由张骞于公元前 114 年左右出使西域时开辟。

海上丝绸之路始于公元前 2 世纪，是连接中国、印度洋流域国家、埃及与欧洲的海洋贸易网络。

新丝绸之路又名“一带一路”，是中国国家主席习近平于 2013 年提出的合作倡议，旨在扩大中国与亚洲其他国家及非洲、欧洲国家的贸易。

《马可·波罗游记》

《马可·波罗游记》是一本描述马可·波罗从 1271 年到 1295 年，从欧洲到亚洲旅行经历的书籍，由马可·波罗口述，鲁思蒂谦记录。书中重点描述了他在忽必烈统治的朝廷中的经历。

该书对于哥伦布、达伽马等欧洲后来的探险家影响重大，促使他们下定决心坐船出海到亚洲。

讨论

1. 为什么马可·波罗不远万里来到中国？

2. 马可·波罗到访中国对促进东西方文化交流有什么影响？

XVIII ZHENG HE TO THE WESTERN OCEAN

Introduction

Zheng He (1371–1433) was a Chinese mariner and diplomat during China's early Ming Dynasty. He was originally named as Ma He, and later adopted the conferred surname Zheng from Emperor Yongle. From 1405 to 1433, Zheng He made seven expeditionary voyages to Southern Asia, Western Asia, and Eastern Africa.

◎ The Chinese woodblock print of Zheng He's voyage, made in the early 17th century

Story Time

In 1405 when Emperor Yongle of the Ming Dynasty intended to expand the trade between China and the countries along the Indian Ocean basin, he appointed Zheng He commander in chief of a series of expeditions to the Western Ocean.

The fleet's first international visit was Champa (in present Vietnam). From there, they went all the way to the Andaman and Nicobar Islands of India. In 1407, they returned to China, laden with tributes and envoys from these states.

After paying their tribute and receiving gifts from the Chinese emperor, the foreign envoys needed to go back to their homes. Therefore, later in 1407, the great fleet set sail once again, carrying these envoys back and going as far as Ceylon (present Sri Lanka) with stops including Champa, Java of Indonesia, and Siam (present Thailand). Zheng He's fleet returned in 1409 with full of fresh tributes and again turned right back for another two-year voyage (1409–1411). This third voyage terminated at Calicut (in present India).

Two years later, the fleet set out on the fourth expedition. They went all the way to the Arabian Peninsula and the Horn of Africa, making port calls including Hormuz, Aden and Mogadishu. He returned to China with exotic goods and creatures, famously including giraffes.

⊙ The painting of a giraffe tribute, made by Chen Zhang of the Ming Dynasty in 1414

On the fifth and sixth voyages, the fleet followed much the same track to Arabia and East Africa, asserting Chinese prestige and collecting tribute from as many as 30 different states. The fifth voyage spanned 1417 to 1419, while the sixth took place between 1421 and 1422.

In 1431, Zheng He set out on his last voyage, which took three years and visited at least 17 different ports between Champa and Kenya. Two years later, Zheng He died of illness on the way back to China, buried in present Indonesian waters.

Cultural Links

The flourishing age of Yongle

During the Ming Dynasty (1368–1644), China exerted immense cultural and political influence on Southeast Asia, West Asia and East Africa.

Emperor Yongle (1360–1424) was the third emperor of the Ming Dynasty. The historical period under his reign was described as the flourishing age of Yongle. His outstanding contributions included forging trade relations with the countries along the Indian Ocean through voyages led by Zheng He to these countries, moving the capital back to Beiping (present Beijing), constructing the Forbidden City, rebuilding the Grand Canal, and expanding the imperial examination system.

⊙ The picture of Emperor Yongle, held by the Palace Museum in Taipei

Christopher Columbus

Christopher Columbus was an Italian explorer, navigator and colonizer. Born in the Republic of Genoa, under the sponsorship of the Catholic Monarchs of Spain, he completed four voyages across the Atlantic Ocean and managed to reach the Americas between 1492 and 1502. Those voyages and his efforts to establish settlements on the island of Hispaniola initiated the European colonization of the New World.

⊙ The model of the Chinese treasure ship

Chinese treasure ship

The Chinese treasure ship was a type of large wooden ship in the fleet of Zheng He, who led seven voyages during the early 15th century. The dimensions of the largest treasure ships were 148 meters by 60 meters, which made them at least twice as long as the largest European ships at the end of the 16th century. Moreover, the largest treasure ship had a displacement of about 22,800 tons, making it steer smoothly even in stormy weather.

Discussion

1. Why did Emperor Yongle send Zheng He to the Western Ocean?
2. Compare the voyages of Zheng He and Columbus. How did they affect the world differently?

拾捌　郑和下西洋

引

郑和（1371 年—1433 年），明朝初期航海家和外交家。郑和原名马和，后永乐皇帝赐其郑姓，故改名为郑和。郑和在 1405 到 1433 年间七下西洋，足迹遍布南亚、西亚、东非等地。

◎ 描绘郑和下西洋的雕版印刷画
17世纪初绘制

故事

1405年，明朝永乐帝为扩大中国与印度洋流域国家的贸易，派郑和率船队下西洋。

郑和船队访问的第一站为占城（今越南境内），然后继续西行到达印度安达曼－尼科巴群岛。1407年，郑和随同这些国家的使臣和朝贡礼品回国。

来到中国后，各国使臣向永乐帝朝贡，永乐皇帝回赠他们礼物，以示友好。而后，各国使臣准备回国。于是，郑和于当年再次出航，护送各国使臣回国，并走访占城、印尼爪哇岛、暹罗（今泰国）等地，最后到达锡兰（今斯里兰卡）。1409年，郑和又带了一批使臣和朝贡礼品回国。之后，郑和第三次下西洋，这次航行最远到访卡利卡特（今印度境内）历时两年（1409年—1411年）。

两年后，郑和第四次出航。这次他们途经阿拉伯半岛和非洲之角，并访问霍尔木兹岛、亚丁湾、摩加迪休等地。郑和回国时带回了包括长颈鹿等异域朝贡礼品。

之后，郑和又进行了第五次（1417年—1419年）和第六次（1421年—1422年）远航。与第四次远航相似，这两次也途径阿拉伯半岛和东非地区。每到一处，

异国贡品麒麟（长颈鹿）
明朝画家陈璋1414年绘

郑和便宣扬明朝国力强盛，并代表明朝接受多达 30 个国家的朝贡。

1431 年，郑和第七次也是最后一次下西洋，走访从占城到肯尼亚沿线至少17个国家。两年后，郑和在回途中病逝，其随行将其海葬于印尼海域。

文化链接

永乐盛世

明朝（1368 年—1644 年）时期，中国对东南亚、西亚和东非有着重要的政治和文化影响。

永乐皇帝（1360 年—1424 年）是明朝第三任皇帝，其统治的时期被称为“永乐盛世”。他的主要功绩包括派遣郑和下西洋、大力发展与别国的经贸关系、迁都北平（今北京）、建造紫禁城、治理大运河和进一步发展科举制。

◎ 永乐皇帝画像
中国台北故宫博物院藏品

克里斯托弗·哥伦布

克里斯托弗·哥伦布是意大利探险家、航海家和殖民者，出生于热那亚共和国。在西班牙的天主教君主的赞助下，他在 1492 年到 1502 年间四次横渡大西洋，并且成功到达美洲。他的这些航行以及在伊斯帕尼奥拉岛创建居民点的努力，拉开了欧洲殖民“新大陆”的序幕。

◎ 宝船模型

宝船

15 世纪初郑和七下西洋，他所率领的舰队中的木制大船就是宝船。其中最大的船只尺寸规格为长 148 米，宽 60 米，比 16 世纪末欧洲最大的船只大了至少两倍。同时，最大的船只排水量约为 22,800 吨，使其能在恶劣的天气中平稳航行。

讨论

1. 永乐帝为什么派郑和下西洋？
2. 比较郑和和哥伦布的航行，其分别对世界产生了哪些不同的影响？

XIX THE STORY OF *KANGXI DICTIONARY*

Introduction

There have been many official efforts throughout China's history to standardize the characters, among which the *Kangxi Dictionary* was a milestone.

It applied the earlier *Zihui* radical system, presently known as 214 Kangxi radicals. A total of 47,035 characters were divided among the radicals, which made it much easier to look up the characters.

The *Kangxi Dictionary* is the first classic book named with "dictionary" in China's history.

◎ *Kangxi Dictionary*, held by the Chinese Dictionary Museum of the Huangcheng Chancellor in Jincheng in Shanxi Province

Story Time

In 1661, Emperor Kangxi (1654–1722) came to the throne in the Qing Dynasty, who was much interested in reading and usually needed to look up Chinese characters. In the Kangxi Era, there were two dictionaries in general, of which one was edited in Manchu language and the other in Han language. Emperor Kangxi yet was dissatisfied with them and also considered them unfavorable factors for the cultural prosperity and integrity in China.

After years of conflicts and warfare, in 1710, Emperor Kangxi started to discuss the way to govern and rule the nation, especially in better Man-Han cultural exchange. Meanwhile, he decided to compile the largest and most comprehensive dictionary of Chinese characters to unite the phonetics, characters and meanings. The officials in the royal court agreed with Emperor Kangxi, particularly Zhang Yushu and Chen Tingjing. After in-depth thoughts, Emperor Kangxi finally directed Zhang Yushu and Chen Tingjing to be in charge of the compilation as editors-in-chief.

Unfortunately, Zhang Yushu passed away soon during the very early phase of his compilation, whose work was continued by Chen Tingjing. Emperor Kangxi usually came to visit the workplace where Chen Tingjing concentrated on his compilation of *Kangxi Dictionary*.

◉ The picture of Emperor Kangxi, displayed at the Palace Museum in Beijing

Kangxi Dictionary was eventually completed in 1716. After his completion, as an editor-in-chief, Chen Tingjing handed in this 47,035-Chinese-character and 12-volume *Kangxi Dictionary*. Emperor Kangxi was satisfied with it and then drafted the preface of the book himself.

Afterwards, *Kangxi Dictionary* was in the hands of almost every scholar who came to take part in Chinese imperial examinations.

Cultural Links

High Qing

Emperor Kangxi's sixty-one-year reign, the longest of the Chinese emperors, began an era of the *High Qing*, which marked the peak of the dynasty. It lasted over a century, through the reigns of Emperor Kangxi, Yongzheng and Qianlong.

The Qing Dynasty (1636–1912) was the last imperial dynasty of China.

The renowned classic books in China

Besides *Kangxi Dictionary*, many classic books are the mirrors of the splendid culture of China. Here are three of them.

1) *Yongle Encyclopaedia*

Emperor Yongle of the Ming Dynasty ordered the compilation of the *Yongle Encyclopaedia*, which includes 11,095 handwritten volumes. It covers China's history, geography, literature, art, philosophy, religion, agriculture, astronomy, drama, geology, and other encyclopaedic knowledge prior to the 14th century.

2) *Complete Library in Four Branches of Literature*

The volumes of *Complete Library in Four Branches of Literature* (totally 36,000 volumes) are far larger than those of *Yongle Encyclopaedia*. It covers all types of Chinese literature in circulation up to the reign of Emperor Qianlong.

3) *Dunhuang Manuscripts*

Dunhuang Manuscripts (totally 50,000 volumes) is a collection of documents discovered in Cave 16 of Mogao Cave of Dunhuang in 1907, which entails the ancient manuscripts and copies ranging from the 2nd century to the 14th century.

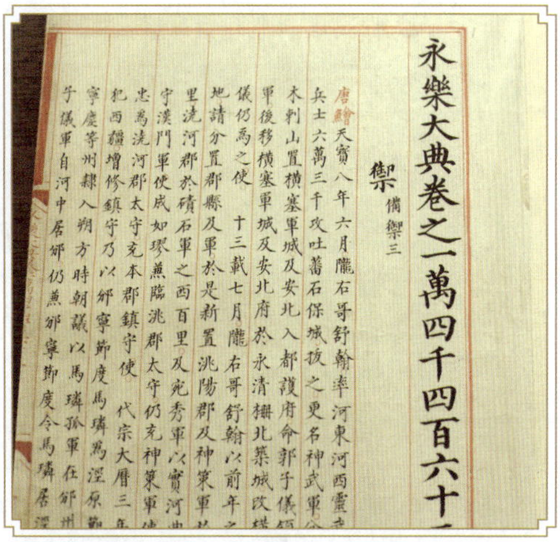

⊙ *Yongle Encyclopaedia*, held by the National Library of China in Beijing

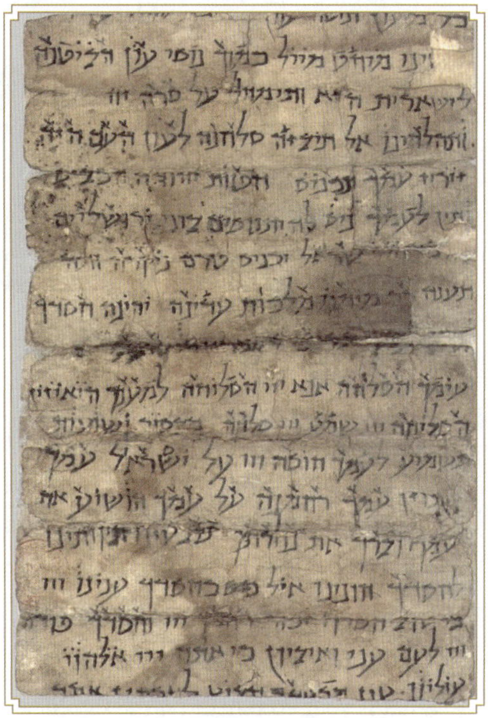

⊙ A leaf from *Dunhuang Manuscripts* written in Hebrew, held by the National Library of France in Paris, France

⊙ A leaf from *Dunhuang Manuscripts* written in Chinese, held by the British Museum in London, the United Kingdom

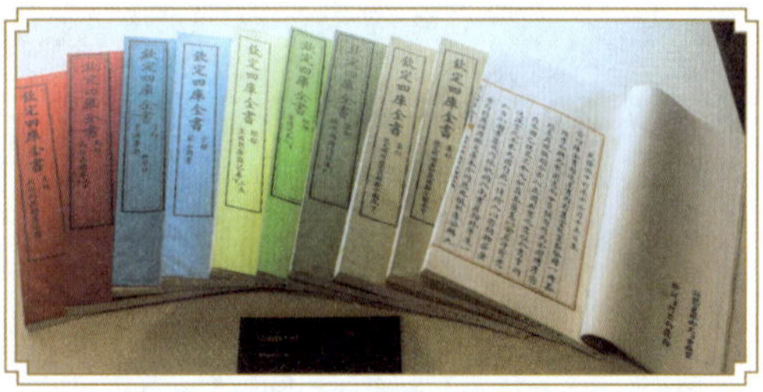

⊙ *Complete Library in Four Branches of Literature*, held by the National Library of China in Beijing

Encyclopaedia Britannica

Encyclopaedia Britannica is the oldest English-language encyclopaedia still in production. It was written by about 100 full-time editors and more than 4,000 contributors, including 110 Nobel Prize winners and five presidents of the United States. *Encyclopaedia Britannica* covers the most influential professions and majors, historical narratives and figures.

Discussion

1. What is your comment on the significance of *Kangxi Dictionary* to Chinese culture?
2. Could you come up with any other Chinese dictionary? Please introduce it.

拾玖 《康熙字典》的故事

引

中国历史上，许多政府都曾努力规范文字。其中，《康熙字典》堪称一座里程碑。

这本字典使用早期《字汇》的部首体系，即现在著名的214个康熙部首。所收录的47,035个汉字按部首进行分类，这种编纂方式使检字更加便捷。

《康熙字典》是中国历史上第一本以“字典”命名的典籍。

◎《康熙字典》
山西晋城皇城相府内中华字典博物馆藏品

故事

1661 年，清朝康熙皇帝（1654 年—1722 年）即位。康熙皇帝痴迷书籍，经常需要查阅字典。在康熙时期，有两部通行字典：一部是满文字典，另一部是汉字字典。可是，康熙对这两部字典并不满意，同时认为其不利于中华文化的繁荣与统一。

1710 年，在经历了重重战乱后，康熙开始商讨治国之道，尤其关注满汉文化的融合。此时，他决心要编纂一部最大、最全的字典，将所有汉字的读音、字形和字义统一起来。这一想法得到了大臣们的拥护，其中张玉书与陈廷敬更是赞同这想法。康熙再三斟酌后，决定任命张玉书与陈廷敬为主编。

◎ 康熙皇帝画像
北京故宫展品

不幸的是，张玉书在编纂初期便过世了，编纂工作由陈廷敬继续完成。康熙时常去陈廷敬编纂字典的地方，发现他编纂得非常认真。

1716 年，这本字典终于编纂完毕。字典分为 12 集，共收录 47,035 个汉字。作为主编的陈廷敬将编好的《康熙字典》呈给了康熙。康熙看完之后觉得很满意，并亲自作序。

此后，凡是进京赶考的读书人，手里皆有一本《康熙字典》。

文化链接

康乾盛世

康熙在位 61 年，是中国所有帝王中在位时间最长的一位皇帝。在其统治期间，中国进入了“康乾盛世”，这也是清朝的巅峰阶段。盛世持续超过一个世纪，历经康熙、雍正到乾隆的统治。

清朝（1636 年—1912 年）是中国最后一个王朝。

著名中国典籍

除了《康熙字典》，还有很多典籍反映了中国的灿烂文化，以下为其中三套。

1）《永乐大典》

明朝永乐皇帝下令手写编纂 11,095 卷《永乐大典》，其内容涵盖了 14 世纪前中华历史、地理、文学、艺术、哲学、宗教、农业、天文学、戏剧、地质学与其他专业学科。

2）《四库全书》

《四库全书》（共 36,000 卷）卷数远超《永乐大典》，囊括了乾隆王朝以前所有的中国文献作品。

3）《敦煌文献》

《敦煌文献》（总约 5 万卷）是 1907 年发现于敦煌莫高窟 16 号洞窟中的一批书籍的总称，包括从公元 2 世纪至 14 世纪的古写本及印本。

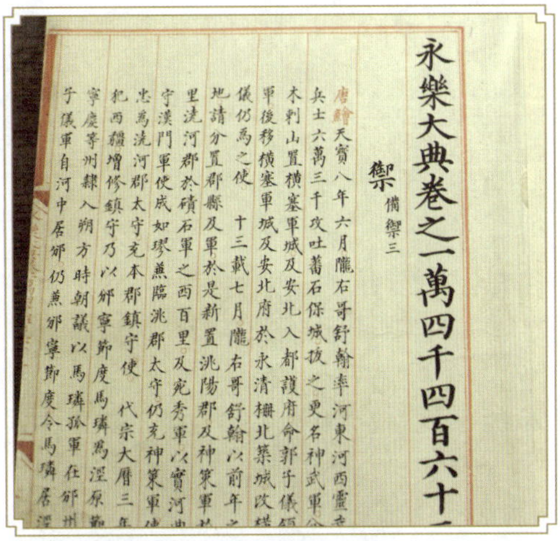
永樂大典卷之一萬四千四百六十

◎《永乐大典》
中国国家图书馆藏品

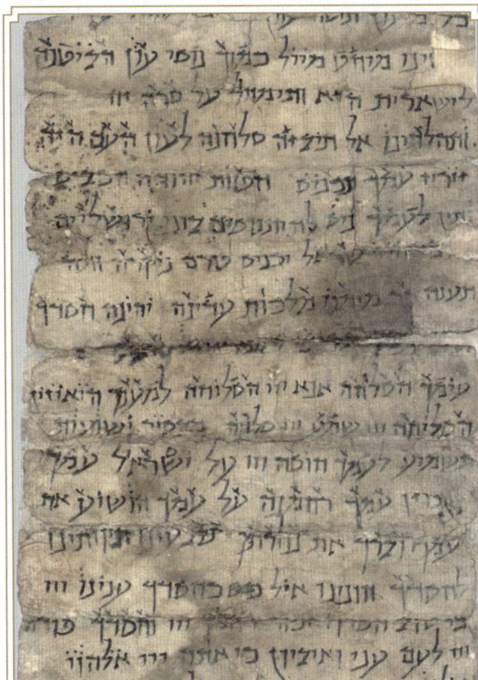

◎ 用希伯来语写的《敦煌文献》书页
法国巴黎的法国国家图书馆藏品

◎ 用中文写的《敦煌文献》书页
英国伦敦的大英博物馆藏品

◎《四库全书》
北京中国国家图书馆藏品

《大英百科全书》

《大英百科全书》是仍在出版的最古老的英语百科全书。约 100 位全职编写者与其他 4000 多位人员共同参与编写，其中包括 110 位诺贝尔奖获得者与 5 位美国总统。《大英百科全书》内容涵盖了各重要领域专业学科、历史叙事以及对重要历史人物之叙述。

讨论

1. 你如何评价《康熙字典》之于中国文化的意义？
2. 你还能想到其他哪些汉语字典？请介绍一下。

XX DESTRUCTION OF OPIUM AT HUMEN

Introduction

Lin Zexu (1785–1850) was a Chinese scholar-official of the Qing Dynasty. He was best known for leading the campaign to destroy the opium at Humen, which demonstrated the great determination of the Chinese people to fight against opium. Lin Zexu is now considered as a national hero in China.

⊙ Lin Zexu supervising the destruction of opium, painted by a Chinese artist of the Qing Dynasty

⊙ The picture of Lin Zexu, painted in 1843

Story Time

In the early 19th century, British merchants smuggled large quantities of illegal opium into China and opium addiction became a serious social problem. Thus, Emperor Daoguang decided to put an end to the opium traffic. In 1839, he appointed Lin Zexu as Imperial Commissioner and sent him to Guangzhou, the hub of the opium traffic.

When Lin Zexu arrived in Guangzhou, he ordered that all foreign opium dealers immediately hand over their opium and cease the traffic. A few days later, these opium dealers convened a meeting, where most of them thought that Lin was such a bluff that they could just pretend to comply with the ban by handing over a small quantity of opium.

However, they underestimated Lin's determination to end the opium traffic. He warned the opium dealers that he would not return to Beijing until the opium was eliminated. With careful planning, Lin Zexu sealed off all the opium dens and prevented access to the port, forcefully cutting off all opium traffic. Three weeks later, the opium dealers finally surrendered all their opium—about 20,000 chests of opium (approximately 1,321 tons).

Lin Zexu then set about destroying the opium. Beginning on 3 June 1839, 500 soldiers worked for 23 days to destroy it, mixing the opium with lime and salt and throwing it into the sea outside of Humen Town. When the task was finished, the American missionary, Elijah Coleman Bridgman, who witnessed the whole process, wrote, "The degree of care and faithfulness, with which the whole work was conducted, far exceeded our expectations."

Knowing Lin Zexu's achievement, Emperor Daoguang was extremely pleased and commented, "There is no joy like that of the destruction of the opium."

◎ The Opium Destruction Pool, located at Humen Town in Guangdong Province

Cultural Links

Illustrated Treatise on the Maritime Kingdoms

The book *Illustrated Treatise on the Maritime Kingdoms*, the first Chinese masterpiece on the West, was based on initial research carried out by Lin Zexu. It was mainly written by Wei Yuan, containing numerous maps and many details in history, geography, science and technology of the world.

Although the book received little attention in China when it was published, it had a profound impact on Japan. More and more Japanese scholars and political reformers became convinced that Japan should open borders to the West. As Liang Qichao, a famous Chinese reformer, said the book had a great influence on the 1868 Meiji Restoration.

◎ The Statue of Lin Zexu in New York City, inscribed with the characters of "PIONEER IN THE WAR AGAINST DRUGS" on its base

Emperor Yongzheng banning opium

Emperor Yongzheng (1678–1735) also realized the hazards of opium. In 1729, he issued regulations on opium prohibition, which turned out to be the first legal regulations against drug in the world.

The regulations prohibited the traffic of opium with the punishments ranging from wearing a cangue to death penalty.

International Day against Drug Abuse and Illicit Trafficking

In December of 1987, the General Assembly decided to set 26 June—the day when the destruction of opium at Humen was completed—as the International Day against Drug Abuse and Illicit Trafficking to strengthen action and cooperation in order to achieve the goal of an international society free of drug abuse.

Discussion

1. Why did Emperor Daoguang decide to ban the opium?
2. What can we do to create a world free of drug abuse?

廿　虎门销烟

引

林则徐（1785 年—1850 年），中国清朝大臣，因领导虎门销烟而闻名。虎门销烟运动彰显了中华民族抵御鸦片的坚定意志。如今，林则徐被誉为中华民族英雄。

◎ 林则徐督查销烟
清朝中国画家画作

◎ 林则徐画像
1843年绘制

故事

19世纪初，大量鸦片经英国商贩流入中国，鸦片已成为当时社会的一大毒瘤。因此，道光帝决定禁止鸦片交易。1839年，道光帝封林则徐为钦差大臣，并派其前往当时鸦片贩卖的老巢广州禁烟。

林则徐一抵达广州，便下令所有外国鸦片商贩立即上缴鸦片，并停止贩卖鸦片。几日后，鸦片商贩密会商讨对策。大多数商贩臆断林则徐只是虚张声势，只要假意顺从，象征性地交点鸦片就行。

然而，他们低估了林则徐禁烟的决心。林则徐警告道，鸦片一日不绝，便一日不回。经过精密筹划，林则徐下令查封广州所有烟馆，封锁港口，取缔鸦片交易。三周后，鸦片商贩最终将鸦片全部上缴。此次共收缴鸦片2万余箱（约1321吨）。

收缴完毕后，林则徐开始准备销烟。他率领500将士将鸦片与石灰、食盐混合，倒入虎门外的大海中。此次销烟从1839年6月3日开始，历时23天。美国传教士裨治文在目睹了销烟全过程后写道：“清军在工作进行时，其细心和忠实的程度远远超过我们的预料。”

虎门销烟的消息传到京城，道光皇帝欣喜万分，说道：“可称大快人心！”

◎ 销烟池
位于广东虎门镇

文化链接

《海国图志》

《海国图志》基于林则徐收集的资料，是中国第一部有关西方世界的著作。此书主要由魏源编写，书中包含大量地图和许多当时世界历史、地理与科技的细节信息。

尽管该书付梓后在国内并未引起重视，但却对日本影响深远。越来越多的日本学者和维新派人士意识到日本需要向西方世界开放。正如中国著名主张变革人士梁启超所言，此书对1868年的明治维新产生了巨大影响。

◎ 纽约市的林则徐雕塑
底座刻有“世界禁毒先驱”字样

雍正帝禁烟

雍正帝（1678年—1735年）在位时也意识到了鸦片的危害。1729年，他颁布禁烟条例。该条例也是全球第一部成文的禁烟条例。

该条例明令禁止鸦片交易，违反条例者轻则枷刑，重则处斩。

国际禁毒日

1987 年 12 月，联大会议决定以中国历史上虎门销烟结束的日期，即 6 月 26 日，定为国际禁止毒品滥用和非法贩运日（简称“国际禁毒日”），加强行动与合作，建设无毒品滥用的国际社会。

讨论

1. 道光帝为什么下令禁烟?
2. 为使全世界没有毒品滥用，我们该怎么做?